REGENTS RESTORATION DRAMA SERIES

General Editor: John Loftis

THE PLAIN DEALER

WILLIAM WYCHERLEY

The Plain Dealer

Edited by

LEO HUGHES

UNIVERSITY OF NEBRASKA PRESS · LINCOLN

Publishers on the Plains
UNP

MANUFACTURED IN THE UNITED STATES OF AMERICA

Regents Restoration Drama Series

The Regents Restoration Drama Series, similar in objectives and format to the Regents Renaissance Drama Series, will provide soundly edited texts, in modern spelling, of the more significant English plays of the late seventeenth and early eighteenth centuries. The word "Restoration" is here used ambiguously and must be explained. If to the historian it refers to the period between 1660 and 1685 (or 1688), it has long been used by the student of drama in default of a more precise word to refer to plays belonging to the dramatic tradition established in the 1660's, weakening after 1700, and displaced in the 1730's. It is in this extended sense—imprecise though justified by academic custom—that the word is used in this series, which will include plays first produced between 1660 and 1737. Although these limiting dates are determined by political events, the return of Charles II (and the removal of prohibitions against the operation of theaters) and the passage of Walpole's Stage Licensing Act, they enclose a period of dramatic history having a coherence of its own in the establishment, development, and disintegration of a tradition.

Each text in the series is based on a fresh collation of the seventeenth- and eighteenth-century editions that might be presumed to have authority. The textual notes, which appear above the rule at the bottom of each page, record all substantive departures from the edition used as the copy-text. Variant substantive readings among contemporary editions are listed there as well. Editions later than the eighteenth century are referred to in the textual notes only when an emendation originating in some one of them is received into the text. Variants of accidentals (spelling, punctuation, capitalization) are not recorded in the notes. Contracted forms of characters' names are silently expanded in speech prefixes and stage directions, and, in the case of speech prefixes, are regularized. Additions to the stage directions of the copy-text are enclosed in brackets. Stage directions such as "within" or "aside" are enclosed in parentheses when they occur in the copy-text.

Spelling has been modernized along consciously conservative lines, but within the limits of a modernized text the linguistic quality of the original has been carefully preserved. Contracted preterites have regularly been expanded. Punctuation has been brought into accord with modern practices. The objective has been to achieve a balance between the pointing of the old editions and a system of punctuation which, without overloading the text with exclamation marks, semicolons, and dashes, will make the often loosely flowing verse and prose of the original syntactically intelligible to the modern reader. Dashes are regularly used only to indicate interrupted speeches, or shifts of address within a single speech.

Explanatory notes, chiefly concerned with glossing obsolete words and phrases, are printed below the textual notes at the bottom of each page. References to stage directions in the notes follow the admirable system of the Revels editions, whereby stage directions are keyed, decimally, to the line of the text before or after which they occur. Thus, a note on 0.2 has reference to the second line of the stage direction at the beginning of the scene in question. A note on 115.1 has reference to the first line of the stage direction following line 115 of the text of the relevant scene. Speech prefixes, and any stage directions attached to them, are keyed to the first line of accompanying dialogue.

JOHN LOFTIS

Stanford University

Contents

List of Abbreviations

DLC   Library of Congress
DFo   Folger Shakespeare Library
ICN   Newberry Library
ICU   University of Chicago Library
om.   omitted

Q1   First Quarto, 1677
Q2   Second Quarto (two states), second edition, 1677
Q3   Third Quarto (two states), third edition, 1681
Q4   Fourth Quarto, fourth edition, 1686
Q5   Fifth Quarto, fifth edition, 1691
Q6   Sixth Quarto, sixth edition, 1694
Q7   Seventh Quarto, seventh edition, 1700
Q8   Eighth Quarto, "sixth" [eighth] edition, 1709
O   Octavo, 1712

Introduction

The text of *The Plain Dealer* presents no grave problems and no complex or intriguing history. As the title page of the first edition informs us, it was licensed on January 9, 1676/77. It was printed by T. N., who can be safely identified as Thomas Newcomb, for James Magnes and Richard Bentley.[1] It was entered in the *Term Catalogue* for the Easter term May 28, 1677. Having won the approval of the audience, it was ready for a second edition before the year was out. And with this second edition arises the first bit of confusion which has marked the history of its printing. The first modern editor to collate the several editions appearing in Wycherley's lifetime was G. B. Churchill, who edited this play and *The Country Wife* for Ginn's Belles Lettres series in 1924. Professor Churchill's industry—he collated all the quartos and octavos he could find—was matched by his excessive caution, which led him to identify two slightly different states of the second and third editions as separate quartos, an error which I hope to correct by this account. In preparing the second edition, Magnes and Bentley's printer, no longer identified on the title page, followed the common practice of compressing the type so that this and all subsequent quartos have 83 pages of text in contrast with the first, which has 96. This edition is listed, as "the second edition," in the *Term Catalogue* for Michaelmas, November 26, 1677. It exists in two states, one (Churchill's Q2) with title page dated 1677 and no indication of edition number, the other (Churchill's Q3) dated 1678 and labeled "second edition." Aside from these the only variations are in the outside forme of Signature G, which seems to

[1] Richardson Pack, in *Some Memoirs of William Wycherley, Esq.* (London, 1724), p. 187, tells how "the bookseller who printed his *Plain-Dealer*" turned the author down when he requested a mere £20 while in debtors' prison. Willard Connely turns Pack's account into something more detailed and dramatic: ". . . Wycherley asked the man for twenty pounds. Magnes turned his back" (*Brawny Wycherley* [New York, 1930], pp. 184–185). Since all this happened in 1682 and James Magnes died in 1679, we are not encouraged to accept this most recent and detailed biography as uniformly trustworthy.

have been opened for revision, and a dropped letter restored in Sig. L2 verso. The third edition also exists in at least two states, variations being confined to title pages. One title page (Churchill's Q4) reads "third edition," 1677; the other (Churchill's Q5) reads "third edition," 1681. Since the publishers are now R. Bentley and M. Magnes and since M. Magnes's name appears in the *Term Catalogue* for the first time in Easter, 1679, the date 1677 is clearly in error. Churchill's extra quartos disappear in this accounting and it is possible to label the successive editions with matching quarto numbers, until the very last one. Dated 1709, it follows Q7 (Churchill's Q9), which is dated 1700 and properly labeled "seventh edition"; yet it is called "the sixth edition" on the title page instead of the eighth.

Churchill's account includes three octavo editions within Wycherley's lifetime but of these only his O3 warrants inclusion as having any authority. (This edition is therefore referred to simply as "O" in the List of Abbreviations and textual notes.) His O1 and O2, dated conjecturally 1710 and 1711, turn out on closer examination to be from the shop of Thomas Johnson, who for more than a quarter of a century carried on his publishing business at the Hague. H. L. Ford disposed of Johnson thirty years ago.[2] Though many of the plays in his "Collections of the Best English Plays" bear the imprint London and are often said to be "Printed for the Company of Booksellers," Ford could find no evidence that a single play had issued from a London shop.

Churchill's O3, which was issued separately in 1712 and used in the first edition of *The Works of the Ingenious Mr. William Wycherley*, 1713, is quite another matter. It follows Q1 far more closely than any of the later quartos do. On the other hand it retains too many of the careless slips which crept into the later quartos to merit consideration as a suitable text.

Since no later issue of the play shows convincing signs of the author's having concerned himself with emendation,[3] I have adopted

[2] *Shakespeare 1700–1740: a Collation of the Editions and Separate Plays with Some Account of T. Johnson and R. Walker* (Oxford, 1935), pp. 46–56. Dr. Giles Dawson, who has also studied the career and productions of Johnson, assures me that Ford's appraisal is essentially correct.

[3] Professor Case attempts to justify his adoption of Churchill's Q3 as copy-text for the play in *British Dramatists from Dryden to Sheridan*, ed. G. H. Nettleton and A. E. Case (Boston, 1939), p. 930, but his decision seems based on his having been misled by Churchill in a few instances and his having misread Churchill in some others.

Q1 as my copy-text and collated with it all the quartos and the one octavo which has any authority. The few emendations from later editions which I have accepted seemed more correct or intelligible than the readings of Q1.

The stage history of *The Plain Dealer* having been set forth in detail in recent years,[4] the merest sketch will suffice here. Though precise dates and figures are not available, there seems little doubt that Wycherley's last play was highly popular for half a century after its first performance. If we may rely on John Dennis—and he claims unimpeachable authority—the play had help at the start. In a paragraph in *Decay and Defects of Dramatick Poetry* (1725?) he describes the activities of several courtiers—Buckingham, Rochester, Dorset, Mulgrave, Savil, Buckley, Denham, Waller—who in effect directed public taste. "And when upon the representations of the *Plain Dealer*, the town, as the author has often told me, appeared doubtful what judgment to form of it, the forementioned gentlemen by their loud approbation of it gave it both a sudden and a lasting reputation."[5] Before the middle of the next century, however, it was found to be too highly seasoned a dish for a public demanding increasingly blander fare. Like the works of Wycherley's contemporaries Etherege and Congreve and Vanbrugh, or like Wycherley's even more salacious *The Country Wife*, it was, as a mid-century critic put the case, speaking of the last-named play, "judged unfit for the present correct taste of the town."[6] So smug an attitude should have warned Garrick that adapting the play would hardly justify the effort, but the attempt was made, by the highly successful dramatist Isaac Bickerstaff. After one season, 1765–1766, his bowdlerized version was almost completely laid aside and, after one last hopeless attempt by John Philip Kemble to revive it in 1796, Wycherley's play was allowed to pass from the stage.

[4] See Emmett L. Avery, "The Reputation of Wycherley's Comedies as Stage Plays in the Eighteenth Century," and "*The Plain Dealer* in the Eighteenth Century," *Research Studies of the State College of Washington*, XII (1944), 129–137, 234–256; also *The London Stage, 1660–1800*, ed. William Van Lennep, Emmett L. Avery, Arthur H. Scouten, George Winchester Stone Jr., and Charles Beecher Hogan; Pt. I (Carbondale, Illinois, 1960), p. 253, *et passim*.

[5] *Critical Works of John Dennis*, ed. E. N. Hooker (Baltimore, 1943), II, 277.

[6] *The Public Advertiser*, October 11, 1766.

When Alexander Pope—"my little infallible," as Wycherley liked to call the young poet—published his *Autumn: The Third Pastoral, or Hylas and Aegon* (1709), he dedicated it to the veteran playwright with whom he had formed a strangely volatile friendship.

> Thou, whom the Nine with Plautus' wit inspire,
> The art of Terence, and Menander's fire,
> Whose sense instructs us, and whose humor charms,
> Whose judgment sways us, and whose spirit warms!
> Oh, skill'd in nature! see the hearts of swains,
> Their artless passions and their tender pains.

Some years later the poet felt it necessary to add a more precise identification of his now deceased friend: "Mr. Wycherley, a famous author of comedies, of which the most celebrated were the *Plain-Dealer* and *Country-Wife*. He was a writer of infinite spirit, satire, and wit. The only objection made to him was that he had too much. However, he was followed in the same way by Mr. Congreve; though with a little more correctness." [7]

What Pope and others meant by wit is possibly best illustrated in *The Plain Dealer* by the audacious epistle dedicatory, which even that sworn enemy of Restoration comedy Richard Steele praised as a "masterpiece of raillery" (*Spectator*, No. 266). To savor the "beauty of the inimitable dedication," as Steele characterizes it, it is necessary to know something of the convention. In virtually all other dedications the party addressed is someone with power and—the whole point of the convention—therefore with patronage to dispense. Wycherley's friend Dryden was a masterly dedicator. No one could excel Charles II's laureate in the art of skilful encomium. Dedicators in most cases indulged in the most brazen flattery, professing to see virtue where

---

[7] This note, which first appeared in the 1751 edition of Pope's works, repeats what had become a critical commonplace: the notion that the authors of the great comedies of manners were too exuberant in satirical imagination. Dryden, who referred to Wycherley as early as 1677 as "the author of the *Plain Dealer*, whom I am proud to call my friend," probably started it, in his *Discourse Concerning Satire* (1693) and his *Parallel of Poetry and Painting* (1695). It was echoed in Boyer's *Letters of Wit, Politicks and Morality* (1701) and opposed vigorously by John Dennis, especially in his "Defence of Mr. Wycherley's Characters in the *Plain-Dealer*," in *Letters on Milton and Wycherley* (1721–1722). Later, in the preface to his own adaptation of *The Plain Dealer* entitled *La Prude*, Voltaire professed to know no comedy, ancient or modern, which could match it in wit.

more disinterested writers saw vice, genius where others could discern no glimmer of talent.

It is this convention which the Plain Dealer professes to follow when he addresses himself in mock obeisance to one of the most notorious bawds in a period when lechery thrived.[8] The chief "beauties," to use Steele's term, lie in the equivocations and in the comparisons, expressed and implied. The associations suggested in the very first line by *favor*, a term of venery as well as of patronage, start us off in the proper—which is to say, improper—key. Even more outrageous accidental parallels appear later in the words *procurement* and *design*, to pass over *moving* and *touchstone*. Another form of wit appears in the ironic mock-praise of "known and famous," "the good you have done is unspeakable," "you are, of all public-spirited people, the most necessary, most communicative, most generous and hospitable." The poor adjectives groan under the load of ambiguities. Still another appears in Wycherley's comparisons, strained perhaps but still valid. It is true that both satirists and procurers would be without occupation if suddenly all folly and vice were to disappear. More subtle but also with no little validity is the parallel between bawdyhouses and playhouses, made in the form of a proposed "freedom of the house" —free admission to the theater was a traditional right of dramatists— for both places. A century later Sir John Hawkins in his biography of Dr. Johnson called attention to the inevitable "halo of brothels" which surrounded any theater. A final irony turns out to be a double one. Like even more famous ironists in English literature—Swift and the later Samuel Butler come readily to mind—he introduces without warning into a series of statements to be taken contrariwise one which he means most emphatically: "... whatsoever your amorous misfortunes have been, none can charge you with that heinous and worst of women's crimes, hypocrisy."

For here lies a key to *The Plain Dealer*, and its sharpest divergence from its chief source, Molière's *Le Misanthrope*. In the French comedy Alceste, with his puritanical demand for a frankness too exigent for mere mortals, is the chief object of satire; others—the marquises, the prude, even the charming coquette—come in for a milder chastisement. But Wycherley is himself something of a puritan, a John Bull *philosophe* who may not require sainthood in an age of sinners but does

---

8 "As keys to *The Plain Dealer*, the prologue, the ironic dedication, and the motto prefixed to the play are particularly significant" (Thomas H. Fujimura, *The Restoration Comedy of Wit* [Princeton, 1952], p. 147).

not condone sin posing as saintliness. Hence the shift of targets in the English play so that Olivia, who combines the roles of coquette and prude, becomes the chief object of derision. She and her clandestine husband, also guilty of a double betrayal of friendship and trust, come very near the line drawn by Ben Jonson for comedy, which is to "sport with folly, not with crime."[9]

Mention of Wycherley's two great predecessors prompts a fuller examination of sources before we turn to satirical details in the play itself. The liaison with the great English playwright is for much of the play fairly tenuous, that with the French writer closer but far from slavish.

Of English comic dramatists in the period before 1642 Ben Jonson was the acknowledged leader, and his reputation was if anything greater after the Restoration than it had been éarlier. The principal comedies, devoted as they were to realistic problems in the here and now, commanded a greater following than the more romantic pieces of Shakespeare set not in London but in a half-mythical Illyria or scarcely less mythical Athens or Ephesus. Wycherley followed Jonson in the very first of his plays, *Love in a Wood*, a play which begins like *The Alchemist* with a quarrel between two unsavory characters who manage to provide entertainment and exposition simultaneously. Later passages, especially the canting scenes between the delightful hypocrite Gripe and Mrs. Joyner, echo such characters as Tribulation Wholesome of *The Alchemist* and Zeal-of-the-Land Busy of *Bartholomew Fair*. Perhaps closest to our play is *The Silent Woman*, a play which an eighteenth-century visitor from Germany, Von Uffenbach, considered "an incomparable representation of a misanthrope."[10] True, there are striking differences between Manly and Morose, enough at times to obscure the parallels. Morose is, as his name implies, an object of scorn with no redeeming qualities of manly concern for the larger implications of evil. And his particular neurosis shows itself to be narrow, a pathological hatred of noise. Nor is he redeemed in the end, only relieved of his chattering wife and a good share of his fortune as he sullenly withdraws to be, as his nephew mockingly puts it, "as private as you will." Yet there are hints of Wycherley's morose hero in their common neurosis, an ailment the eighteenth century was to dub "the English malady." They resemble each other

[9] Prologue to *Every Man in His Humour*.
[10] *London in 1710: from the Travels of Zacharias Conrad Von Uffenbach*, ed. W. H. Quarrell and Margaret Mare (London, 1934), p. 52.

too in despising the "common forms, as 'God save you' and 'you are welcome'," without which in Freeman's view both friendship and religion are "unnatural and undecent." They even find a common ground of complaint against society as it reveals itself in law, "with the tedious recitals of their lawsuits" (*The Plain Dealer*, I. 448–449), or "with their several voices of citations, appellations, allegations . . . ." (*Silent Woman*, IV.viii. 14–15). What Wycherley derived from Jonson, however, was something more important than hints of a common type of character. For in a good share of the better scenes in *The Plain Dealer*, as I shall try to show in a moment, he imitated the Jonsonian *method*, the device of developing comedy through a display of "humors," of eccentricities which amount almost to obsessions.[11] Jonson developed, in and for a nation which gloried in its freedom to be eccentric, a form of comedy which was to be exploited in later drama, and in the novel as well.

For the Jonsonian manner affected other comic writers after 1660, writers like Shadwell, who never tired of linking his work with Jonson's and whose one persistent claim to originality was that no comedy he presented was without some novel "humors" character, some person in whose makeup a quirk of personality dominated. Like Wycherley, Shadwell borrowed plots and scenes from Molière but, unlike Wycherley, he was always denying his dependence. What Dryden said of Ben Jonson in the *Essay of Dramatic Poesy* might well apply to the author of *The Plain Dealer*: "He invades authors like a monarch; and what would be theft in other poets is only victory in him."[12] Any resemblances between Wycherley and Shadwell in their actual plays are the result of their sharing common sources and a common objective. Actually it is possible to disclaim any influence of another English playwright—other than Jonson—with the possible exception of Shakespeare, whose faithful Viola in *Twelfth Night* anticipates Fidelia, that refugee from romance.

Traces of Molière are numerous in *The Plain Dealer*, yet no character, no scene, no bit of dialogue even, is transplanted without change. The most extensive borrowing is from Molière's greatest comedy, *Le Misanthrope*. Parallels, never quite exact, can be found in the two

11 Alexander H. Chorney, "Wycherley's Manly Reinterpreted," *Essays Critical and Historical Dedicated to Lily B. Campbell* (Berkeley and Los Angeles, 1950), pp. 161–169, traces a lineage for Manly from Timon and Thersites to Earle's Blunt Man.

12 *Essays of John Dryden*, ed. W. P. Ker (Oxford, 1900), I, 82.

principals, both in their views of life and, at the start, their circumstances. Both could bear the name of Jonson's Morose, if not of the even more famous Timon, for both have lineages going back to Lucian and Menander. Olivia combines the coquette Célimène with the prude Arsinoé and still manages to be herself, a far more vicious character than Molière could have conceived. Novel and Plausible are approximations of Acaste and Clitandre. Freeman and Eliza, like Philinte and Éliante, are the representatives of reason, whose more modest expectations of their fellow men contrast sharply with the puritanical requirements of the misanthrope himself. A few scenes are roughly parallel: the opening one of stark character exposition, the letter scene involving the two marquises, in *The Plain Dealer* Novel and Plausible (IV.ii), most striking of all the big scene in the second act in Olivia's lodgings. When Olivia calls out "Chairs there!" an audience familiar with Molière leans forward in expectation of one of the great episodes in manners comedy, the famous *fauteuil* scene.

Little more than hints of other Molière plays appear. The dramatic self-defense of the *Critique of the School for Wives* is followed, in the scene just mentioned, when Olivia attacks and Eliza defends *The Country Wife*. Eliza has her work cut out for her, for Wycherley's play is a bold, unrelieved sketch of contemporary manners alongside which Molière's picture of the ingenuous Agnès is quite pale. More conjectural is the imitation of another of Molière's pieces, *Les Fâcheux*—variously translated as *The Bores* or *The Impertinents*. Any comic writer of Jonson's bent would find this play imitable as it represents little more than the merest bones of dramatic satire: a man of sardonic temperament is exposed to a succession of fools while a witty friend plays both straight man and audience—with an occasional critical fling at the too-exigent first man. Shadwell had used this device in his popular *The Sullen Lovers* (1668), the *dramatis personae* of which reads like a recipe for "humors" comedy: "Stanford, a morose, melancholy man, tormented beyond measure with the impertinence of people and resolved to leave the world to be quit of them; Lovel, an airy young gentleman, friend to Stanford, one that is pleased with and laughs at the impertinents, and that which is the other's torments is his recreation," and so on. Past this pair sitting in review troop a succession of fools to display their various follies. Just such a situation occurs in Act III of *The Plain Dealer*, in the period of relative calm after Freeman has contrived to steal both ward and papers from the widow. Freeman introduces the scene with a question addressed to Manly: "Well, but how, pray, have you passed your time here since I was forced to leave you alone?" After a response which amounts to an accounting for the bores he has already endured, Manly is visited by a succession of new ones, each being allowed to stay long enough to show off his chief folly and then sent on his way, the ruse to get rid of him being based upon his particular folly. In Molière the device serves for a whole comédie-ballet; here it makes a fitting close to the central scene in Westminster Hall.

Other dependences on French authors may exist, but these are the only ones I should care to vouch for. Churchill and others profess to see anticipations of the Widow Blackacre in Racine's litigious widow in Les Plaideurs,[13] but the resemblance is so faint as to be indiscernible. Fluellen's "There is a river in Macedon and there is also moreover a river in Monmouth" should serve as a model—or warning—for the too-ardent seeker after parallels.[14]

Whatever his debts to predecessors, Wycherley wasted no time acknowledging or denying them, in part because he realized that his sophisticated audience would detect them anyway, in part because he shared at least some of his hero's scorn of ceremony—the legend of how his affair with the Duchess of Cleveland began has an altogether plausible ring.[15] Yet the principal reason is that our author's chief interest lay in the attacks on folly; the devices by which he was able to present these were of lesser concern to him.

Which brings us to the topical material in the play—and the universal satire as well. For in spite of all professions of wholesome intentions, all customary disclaimers of hatred for the sinner rather than the sin, the plain truth remains that a basic function of satire is to provide catharsis for the observer rather than therapy for the object of satire. That the supply of Novels and Plausibles, even of

13 The Country Wife and the Plain Dealer, ed. G. B. Churchill (Boston, 1924), p. 190. The connection seems to have first been made by Macaulay in his long review of Leigh Hunt's Comic Dramatists of the Restoration, Complete Writings of Lord Macaulay (Boston, 1900), XV, 78, but it has been rejected by W. C. Ward, William Wycherley (London, 1888), p. 366, and by Montague Summers, The Complete Works of William Wycherley (London, 1924), II, 92.

14 M. J. O'Regan, "Furetière and Wycherley," Modern Language Review, LIII (1958), 77–81, finds sources for a couple of items in both play and dedication in Furetière's Roman Bourgeois.

15 Critical Works, II, 409–412.

Olivias and Vernishes, visibly diminished after 1676 is too much to expect—unless we are all Manlys.

And this in turn brings us to the very large question of plain-dealing as a vocation. Molière clearly considered his plain-dealing Alceste a fool, a man who cast humanity in a role it was unequal to—and then agonized over its failure to meet his expectations. Molière was in time to pay for his plain dealing with plain dealers when Rousseau attacked him, and through him the whole theater, for his harsh treatment of Alceste. Either from conviction or from prudence Wycherley evaded the attacks of people of Rousseau's temper and wound up with what appears to be an attempt to please both sides. That is, he went part of the way in showing Manly's folly in requiring so much of everyone, but in the end he relented by allowing him to reform by accepting the world on its own terms. This striking conversion is brought about by Manly's discovery that there is one person whose virtue is "greater than I thought any was in this world." The fact that this discovery is made at the cost of still another, that the *two* persons he had formerly considered trustworthy are consummate villains, does not appear to have occurred to Manly—or possibly to the author—but it does to us. His moral calculus simply does not come out right.

Dryden considered *The Plain Dealer* to be "one of the most bold, most general, and most useful satires, which has ever been presented on the English theatre."[16] The carefully chosen terms, particularly when we recall Dryden's parallel between his friend and the sardonic Juvenal,[17] prepare us for the severe castigation of vice and folly the play provides, and at the same time prepare us to accept Manly and his plain dealing more favorably than his surly humor would commonly warrant. And there are times when his picture of the age is graced with almost enough wit to make it acceptable. Take, for example, his vignette of "Bays's grand dance" in which the leaders of the business world, the professions, even the clergy "tread 'round in a preposterous huddle of ceremony" (I.299–307). Or his wry comment to Freeman when the latter justifies his pursuit of the widow by calling attention to her wealth: "Ay, but he that marries a widow for her money will find himself as much mistaken as the widow that marries a young fellow for due benevolence, as you call it" (III.473–

[16] *The Author's Apology for Heroic Poetry* (1677), in *Essays*, I, 182.
[17] *A Discourse Concerning the Original and Progress of Satire* (1693), in *Essays*, II, 84–85.

475). In this entire scene, the one in Westminster Hall referred to above as following *Les Fâcheux*, Manly comes near the sort of detachment from his own affairs necessary for wit. For a few moments he seems ready to join the company of such wry commentators on the human scene as Etherege's Medley in *The Man of Mode* and Congreve's Scandal in *Love for Love*.

Yet he soon alienates us with his pride and self-righteousness—"I that can do a rude thing rather than an unjust thing"—with his worse than inconsiderate treatment of his followers who have stood by him in spite of his surliness, with his obtuseness, which causes him to be so taken in by the patent hypocrisy of mistress and friend, with the savagery of his revenge on the woman he had loved.[18] In the long run we are far better pleased with the cooler appraisals of vice and folly provided by those compliers with the age, Freeman and Eliza. Freeman's eagerness to find sport in the conduct of fools is harmless enough since the fools are blissfully unaware of his scorn and grateful for the opportunity to exhibit themselves.

And it is in the parade of follies that such appeal as the play still has must lie. These take up the greater part of the second and third acts, and also the brief scene in the first where the Widow and her "chopping minor" are introduced. Postponing for a moment the Jonsonian scenes in which the Widow Blackacre provides much of the comedy and the motivating force, we ought first to look at the one big scene, comprising all of Act II, which most closely approximates the kind of manners comedy Wycherley's great contemporaries produced: Etherege, Congreve, Dryden—the Dryden, that is, of the comic scenes of *Marriage à la Mode*. Since Olivia has not as yet revealed the depths of her viciousness, it is possible for her to command the center of the stage in this scene of extended raillery, command it in her dual role of prude and railer-in-chief. Some of her speeches are sheer bits of sophistication, with enough wit to counterbalance the basic malice: "She looks like an old coach new painted, affecting an unseemly smugness, whilst she is ready to drop in

18 The two most recent studies of *The Plain Dealer* stress the savagery of Manly. Miss Anne Righter, "William Wycherley," *Restoration Theatre* (London, 1965), pp. 71–91, uses terms like "monomaniac" and "malcontent on a grand and emotional scale," to describe Manly, and "savage spirit" to characterize the whole play. Miss Rose Zimbardo, in a more ambitious and learned but deplorably tendentious study, *Wycherley's Drama* (New Haven, 1965), classifies Manly as "satyr-satirist" and the play as not comedy at all but "formal satire in the dramatic mode."

pieces" (ll. 177–179). "He a wit! Hang him, he's only an adopter of straggling jests and fatherless lampoons, by the credit of which he eats at good tables and so, like the barren beggar-woman, lives by borrowed children" (ll. 251–254). Much of the time, however, we laugh at rather than with Olivia, at her overzealous but futile battle against self-disclosure, at her obtuseness: "Ay, those fops who love to talk all themselves are of all things my aversion" (ll. 239–240).

Yet this scene, like some of Congreve's, provides an opportunity for everyone to be witty. Even Lettice has her delightful litany of women's follies: "For if, by her indiscretion, a lady be talked of for a man, she cries presently, ''Tis a censorious world'." and so on (ll. 14–21). Novel has his moments as a wit and not mere wit-would: "Taking a fool out of one's mouth is worse than taking the bread out of one's mouth" (ll. 233–235). "I cannot stay in any place where I'm not allowed a little Christian liberty of railing" (ll. 264–265). The best lines are assigned, however, to the one admirable character in the scene, Eliza. When Novel protests over Olivia's giving a vicious characterization before she knows who is being traduced, Eliza remarks drily: "No, that is not fair, though it be usual" (l. 228). Again, in an aside, she produces a more elaborate epigram: "So! I find kissing and railing succeed each other with the angry men as well as with the angry women; and their quarrels are like love quarrels, since absence is the only cause of them; for as soon as the man appears again, they are over" (ll. 287–291). Earlier she makes an equally penetrating comment on women's duplicity, this one not in an aside:

> Come, our tongues belie our hearts more than our pocket-glasses do our faces; but methinks we ought to leave off dissembling, since 'tis grown of no use to us; for all wise observers understand us nowadays as they do dreams, almanacs, and Dutch gazettes, by the contrary. And a man no more believes a woman when she says she has an aversion for him than when she says she'll cry out (ll. 89–96).

So important does Eliza become in setting the moral and social tone of the scene, always in sharp opposition to Olivia, that when she departs—to go see *The Country Wife*—the wit evaporates and the serious combat resumes.

The Blackacre scenes are more Jonsonian and even more amusing. Dryden, whom I have repeatedly invoked as the indispensable link between his friend and the earlier master of comedy,[19] calls particular attention, in his famous "Examen of the *Silent Woman*," to a favorite device of Jonson's which he has

> left . . . to us almost as a rule; that is, when he has a character or humor wherein he would show a *coup de maistre*, or his highest skill, he recommends it to your observation by a pleasant description of it before the person first appears . . . . So that before they come upon the stage you have a longing expectation of them, which prepares you to receive them favorably . . . .[20]

Since both Manly and Freeman show by their ready and lengthy response to the sailor-doorkeeper's announcement of Widow Blackacre's arrival that they know her quite well already, the details provided are obviously designed to introduce a *coup de maistre*. And the creation of the litigious widow and her naïve overgrown son is indeed a master stroke. Their connection with the main plot is admittedly tenuous.[21] Yet no one would challenge their claim to almost a quarter of the play.

The comic mode of the Blackacre scenes is as Jonsonian as the device of introducing them. For the widow is a "humors" character, a soul so obsessed by her one interest that she has sacrificed everything—her comfort, her time, her money, her instincts as woman and mother even—to it. Her provincial residence is, by choice, Norfolk, notorious for its litigiousness. Her London residence is the Inns of Chancery, in the very heart of hearts of English law. When she is not busily engaged in her own numerous cases her greatest pleasure is in listening to her precious son reciting hypothetical ones. And mention of the son focuses attention on another triumphant characterization. Any disposition on the part of a modern reader to sympathize with the victim of so possessive a mother is dispelled by the realization that such sympathy would be wasted on Jerry. True, he is growing a

---

[19] At some point during their careers the two actually talked of collaborating. See the interesting miscellany of 1717 which Ault ascribed to Pope's editorship: *Pope's Own Miscellany*, ed. Norman Ault (London, 1935). The very first poem is "An Epistle to Mr. Dryden, from Mr. Wycherley. Occasion'd by His Proposal to Write a Comedy Together."

[20] *Essays*, I, 87.

[21] T. W. Craik calls attention to the "slight connection" between the plots and to what he considers the ineffectual attempts to link them: "Some Aspects of Satire in Wycherley's Plays," *English Studies*, XLI (1960), 168–179.

trifle restless over the unconscionable delay in arriving at man's estate, but meanwhile he has his precious trees and the apostle spoons to console him, forsooth.

And with this hint of the boy's delightful provincial speech we come to a final Jonsonian element, the exuberant rhetoric. Jerry is still in his apprenticeship in legal jargon but the widow has long since been made free of the city. How the words come tumbling out, as when she catalogues Oldfox's weakness—"my walking hospital of an ancient foundation, thou bag of mummy . . . thou withered, hobbling, distorted cripple" (II.864–870) and without pausing for breath wheels about to give Freeman his pedigree. "Hey, brave mother for calling of names, ifac!" (II.877) says Jerry, and we consider the praise well deserved. In her legal canting she is clearly akin to some of the older dramatist's best creations like Zeal-of-the-Land Busy or Sir Epicure Mammon, who pour out words with the same abandon, and she anticipates Congreve's Sir Sampson Legend and Lady Wishfort. It is not hard to understand why Tony Aston, looking for comic scenes with which to spice up his "Medley," should choose the Blackacre scenes for performances in 1744, a full season after Wycherley's play had its last regular performance.[22]

LEO HUGHES

University of Texas

[22] A. H. Scouten, *The London Stage*, Pt. III, ii, 1092, 1096.

THE PLAIN DEALER

Ridiculum acri
Fortius et melius magnas plerumque secat res.
Horat.

Ridicule is commonly more effective in deciding great issues than severity.

Horace *Sat.* I, x, 14–15

1. *acri*] *Q 2–8, O; acre Q 1.*

To My Lady B———

Madam,

   Though I never had the honor to receive a favor from you,
nay, or be known to you, I take the confidence of an author
to write to you a *billet doux* dedicatory, which is no new   5
thing, for by most dedications it appears that authors,
though they praise their patrons from top to toe and seem
to turn them inside out, know them as little as sometimes
their patrons their books, though they read them out; and if
the poetical daubers did not write the name of the man or   10
woman on top of the picture, 'twere impossible to guess
whose it were. But you, Madam, without the help of a poet,
have made yourself known and famous in the world, and,
because you do not want it, are therefore most worthy of an
epistle dedicatory. And this play claims naturally your pro-   15
tection, since it has lost its reputation with the ladies of
stricter lives in the playhouse; and (you know) when men's
endeavors are discountenanced and refused, by the nice
coy women of honor, they come to you, to you the great
and noble patroness of rejected and bashful men, of which   20
number I profess myself to be one, though a poet, a
dedicating poet; to you I say, madam, who have as discerning a judgment, in what's obscene or not, as any quick-
sighted civil person of them all, and can make as much of a
double-meaning saying as the best of them; yet would not,   25
as some do, make nonsense of a poet's jest, rather than not
make it bawdy; by which they show they as little value wit in
a play as in a lover, provided they can bring the other thing
about. Their sense indeed lies all one way, and therefore are
only for that in a poet which is moving, as they say. But   30
what do they mean by that word moving? Well, I must not
put them to the blush, since I find I can do it. In short,
madam, you would not be one of those who ravish a poet's
innocent words, and make them guilty of their own naughti-
ness (as 'tis termed) in spite of his teeth; nay, nothing is   35

---

4. *or*] *Q 1–6, Q 8, O*; *nor Q 7.*   14. *of*] *Q 1–2, O*; *om. Q 3–8.*

---

1. *Lady B*———] Mother Bennet, a notorious London procuress.

secure from the power of their imaginations; no, not their
husbands, whom they cuckold with themselves by thinking
of other men and so make the lawful matrimonial embraces
adultery; wrong husbands and poets in thought and word,
to keep their own reputations. But your ladyship's justice, I 40
know, would think a woman's arraigning and damning a
poet for her own obscenity, like her crying out a rape, and
hanging a man for giving her pleasure, only that she might
be thought not to consent to it; and so to vindicate her
honor forfeits her modesty. But you, madam, have too much 45
modesty to pretend to it; though you have as much to say for
your modesty as many a nicer she, for you never were seen at
this play, no, not the first day; and 'tis no matter what
people's lives have been, they are unquestionably modest
who frequent not this play. For as Mr. Bays says of his, that it 50
is the only touchstone of men's wit and understanding, mine
is, it seems the only touchstone of women's virtue and
modesty. But hold, that touchstone is equivocal, and by the
strength of a lady's imagination may become something that
is not civil; but your ladyship, I know, scorns to misapply a 55
touchstone. And, madam, though you have not seen this
play, I hope (like other nice ladies) you will the rather read
it. Yet, lest the chambermaid or page should not be trusted,
and their indulgence could gain no further admittance for it
than to their ladies' lobbies or outward rooms, take it into 60
your care and protection, for, by your recommendation and
procurement, it may have the honor to get into their closets;
for what they renounce in public often entertains them there,
with your help especially. In fine, madam, for these and
many other reasons, you are the fittest patroness or judge of 65
this play, for you show no partiality to this or that author.
For from some many ladies will take a broad jest as cheer-
fully as from the watermen, and sit at some downright filthy
plays (as they call them) as well satisfied and as still as a

36. imaginations] *Q1–5, Q8, O;*
imagination *Q6–7.*
59. indulgence] *Q1–2, O;* indul-
gences *Q3–8.*

60. rooms] *Q1–3;* room *Q4–8, O.*
69–70. as a poet] *Q1–6, Q8, O;* as
poet *Q7.*

50. *Mr. Bays*] principal object of satire in *The Rehearsal,* 1671.

poet could wish them elsewhere. Therefore it must be the 70
doubtful obscenity of my plays alone they take exceptions
at, because it is too bashful for them; and indeed most
women hate men for attempting to halves on their chastity,
and bawdy I find, like satire, should be home, not to have it
taken notice of. But, now I mention satire, some there are 75
who say, 'tis the plain dealing of the play, not the obscenity;
'tis taking off the ladies' masks, not offering at their petti-
coats, which offends them. And generally they are not the
handsomest, or most innocent, who are the most angry at
being discovered: 80

> —*Nihil est audacius illis*
> *Deprehensis; iram, atque animos a crimine sumunt.*

Pardon, madam, the quotation, for a dedication can no
more be without ends of Latin than flattery; and 'tis no
matter whom it is writ to; for an author can as easily (I 85
hope) suppose people to have more understanding and
languages than they have, as well as more virtues. But why
the devil should any of the few modest and handsome be
alarmed? (For some there are who as well as any deserve
those attributes, yet refrain not from seeing this play, nor 90
think it any addition to their virtue to set up for it in a playhouse, lest there it should look too much like acting.) But
why, I say, should any at all of the truly virtuous be concerned, if those who are not so are distinguished from them?
For by that mask of modesty which women wear promis- 95
cuously in public, they are all alike, and you can no more
know a kept wench from a woman of honor by her looks
than by her dress. For those who are of quality without
honor (if any such there are), they have their quality to set
off their false modesty, as well as their false jewels, and you 100
must no more suspect their countenances for counterfeit than
their pendants, though, as the Plain-dealer Montaigne says,

---

71. plays] *Q 1–8*; play *O*.   82. *iram*] *Q 1–7*; *itam Q 8, O.*
75. taken] *Q 1–6, Q 8, O*; taken any   92. there] *Q 1, O; om. Q 2–8.*
Q 7.

81–82. *Nihil . . . sumunt*] Nothing is bolder than these when found out;
their anger and spirit rise in the same proportion as their guilt (Juvenal,
Satires, VI, 284–285).

Els envoy leur conscience au bordel, & teinnent leur contenance en règle. But those who act as they look, ought not to be scandalized at the reprehension of others' faults, lest they tax 105 themselves with them and by too delicate and quick an apprehension not only make that obscene which I meant innocent, but that satire on all, which was intended only on those who deserved it. But, madam, I beg your pardon for this digression to civil women and ladies of honor, since you 110 and I shall never be the better for them. For a comic poet and a lady of your profession make most of the other sort, and the stage and your houses, like our plantations, are propagated by the least nice women. And, as with the ministers of justice, the vices of the age are our best business. 115 But, now I mention public persons, I can no longer defer doing you the justice of a dedication, and telling you your own, who are, of all public-spirited people, the most necessary, most communicative, most generous and hospitable. Your house has been the house of the people, your sleep 120 still disturbed for the public, and when you arose 'twas that others might lie down, and you waked that others might rest. The good you have done is unspeakable. How many young unexperienced heirs have you kept from rash, foolish marriages and from being jilted for their lives by the worst 125 sort of jilts, wives? How many unbewitched widowers' children have you preserved from the tyranny of stepmothers? How many old dotards from cuckoldage and keeping other men's wenches and children? How many adulteries and unnatural sins have you prevented? In fine, 130 you have been a constant scourge to the old lecher, and often a terror to the young. You have made concupiscence its own punishment, and extinguished lust with lust, like blowing up of houses to stop the fire.

---

103. *Els envoy*] *Q1, O; Elles envoyent Q2; Eles envoyent Q3–8.*
103. *contenance*] *Q1–6; countenance*

Q7; continence Q8, O.
128. dotards] *Q1–7;* doaters *Q8, O.*

103–104. *Els . . . règle*] They send their consciences to the stews, and keep a starched countenance (Montaigne, *Works*, tr. Cotton, Vol. IV, *Essays* [London, 1923], Bk. III, Ch. 5, p. 262). The other quotations from Montaigne in the Dedication are also cited from Bk. III, Ch. 5, of this edition.

Nimirum propter continentiam, incontinentia   135
Necessaria est, incendium ignibus extinguitur.

There's Latin for you again, madam. I protest to you, as
I am an author, I cannot help it. Nay, I can hardly keep
myself from quoting Aristotle and Horace, and talking to
you of the rules of writing (like the French authors), to show 140
you and my readers I understand them in my epistle lest
neither of you should find it out by the play; and, according
to the rules of dedications, 'tis no matter whether you
understand or no what I quote or say to you of writing, for
an author can as easily make anyone a judge or critic in an 145
epistle as an hero in his play. But, madam, that this may
prove to the end a true epistle dedicatory, I'd have you
know 'tis not without a design upon you which is in the
behalf of the fraternity of Parnassus, that songs and sonnets
may go at your houses and in your liberties for guineas 150
and half guineas, and that wit, at least with you, as of old,
may be the price of beauty. And so you will prove a true
encourager of poetry, for love is a better help to it than
wine, and poets, like painters, draw better after the life than
by fancy. Nay, in justice, madam, I think a poet ought to be 155
as free of your houses as of the playhouses, since he contri-
butes to the support of both and is as necessary to such as
you as a ballad-singer to the pick-purse, in convening the
cullies at the theaters, to be picked up and carried to supper
and bed at your houses. And, madam, the reason of this 160
motion of mine is, because poor poets can get no favor in the
tiring rooms, for they are no keepers, you know; and folly
and money, the old enemies of wit, are even too hard for it
on its own dunghill. And for other ladies, a poet can least go
to the price of them. Besides, his wit, which ought to recom- 165
mend him to them, is as much an obstruction to his love as
to his wealth or preferment, for most women nowadays

---

141. readers] *Q1*; reader *Q2–8, O.*   159. to supper] *Q1–2, O*; to a
supper *Q3–8.*

135–136. *Nimirum . . . extinguitur*] Forsooth incontinency is necessary for
continency's sake; a conflagration is extinguished by fire (*Essays*, p. 279).
Wycherley almost certainly took the quotation from Montaigne, who took
it from Tertullian.

apprehend wit in a lover as much as in a husband. They
hate a man that knows them. They must have a blind, easy
fool whom they can lead by the nose and, as the Scythian 170
women of old, must baffle a man and put out his eyes ere
they will lie with him, and then too, like thieves, when they
have plundered and stripped a man, leave him. But if there
should be one of a hundred of those ladies generous enough
to give herself to a man that has more wit than money (all 175
things considered) he would think it cheaper coming to you
for a mistress though you made him pay his guinea, as a man
in a journey (out of good husbandry) had better pay for what
he has in an inn than lie on freecost at a gentleman's house.

In fine, madam, like a faithful dedicator I hope I have 180
done myself right in the first place, then you and your profession, which in the wisest and most religious government
of the world, is honored with the public allowance, and in
those that are thought the most uncivilized and barbarous
is protected and supported by the ministers of justice. And 185
of you, madam, I ought to say no more here, for your virtues
deserve a poem rather than an epistle or a volume entire to
give the world your memoirs or life at large, and which
(upon the word of an author that has a mind to make an
end of his dedication) I promise to do, when I write the 190
annals of our British love, which shall be dedicated to the
ladies concerned, if they will not think them something too
obscene too, when your life, compared with many that are
thought innocent, I doubt not may vindicate you, and me,
to the world for the confidence I have taken in this address 195
to you, which then may be thought neither impertinent, nor
immodest. And, whatsoever your amorous misfortunes have
been, none can charge you with that heinous and worst of
women's crimes, hypocrisy. Nay, in spite of misfortunes or
age you are the same woman still, though most of your sex 200
grow Magdalens at fifty and, as a solid French author has it,

> Apres le plaisir, vien't la peine,
> Apres la peine la vertu.

179. than] *Q1-7, O*; then *Q8*.   183. of] *Q1-7*; in *Q8, O*.

170–171. *Scythian women*] *Essays*, p. 290.
202–203. *Apres le plaisir . . . vertu.*] After pleasure, pain; after pain
virtue. The epigram is evidently proverbial.

But sure an old sinner's continency is much like a gamester's forswearing play when he has lost all his money. And 205
modesty is a kind of a youthful dress, which as it makes a
young woman more amiable makes an old one more
nauseous. A bashful old woman is like an hopeful old man,
and the affected chastity of antiquated beauties is rather a
reproach than an honor to them, for it shows the men's vir- 210
tue only, not theirs. But you, in fine, madam, are no more
an hypocrite than I am when I praise you. Therefore I
doubt not will be thought (even by yours and the play's
enemies, the nicest ladies) to be the fittest patroness for,

Madam,   215

Your ladyship's most obedient,

faithful, humble servant, and

THE PLAIN DEALER

205. has] *Q 1–2*; had *Q 3–8, O.*

___

PROLOGUE

Spoken by the Plain Dealer

I, the Plain Dealer, am to act today.
And my rough part begins before the play.
First, you who scribble, yet hate all that write,
And keep each other company in spite,
As rivals in your common mistress, fame,   5
And with faint praises one another damn;
'Tis a good play (we know) you can't forgive,
But grudge yourselves the pleasure you receive:
Our scribbler therefore bluntly bid me say,
He would not have the wits pleased here today.   10
Next, you, the fine, loud gentlemen of the pit,
Who damn all plays; yet, if y'ave any wit,
'Tis but what here you sponge, and daily get;
Poets, like friends to whom you are in debt,
You hate: and so rooks laugh, to see undone   15
Those pushing gamesters whom they live upon.
Well, you are sparks; and still will be i'th' fashion:
Rail then, at plays, to hide your obligation.
Now, you shrewd judges who the boxes sway,
Leading the ladies' hearts, and sense astray,   20
And, for their sakes, see all, and hear no play;
Correct your cravats, foretops, lock behind,
The dress and breeding of the play ne'er mind:
Plain dealing is, you'll say, quite out of fashion;
You'll hate it here, as in a dedication.   25
And your fair neighbors, in a limning poet,
No more than in a painter will allow it.
Pictures too like, the ladies will not please:
They must be drawn too here, like goddesses.
You, as at Lely's too, would truncheon wield,   30

9. bluntly bid me] *Q 1–7, O*; bid me
bluntly *Q 8*.

---

13. *sponge*] not, as often glossed, because they avoid paying admission,
but because they pick up repartee from plays to grace their own speech.
   26. *limning poet*] metaphorically, a writer who draws satirical portraits.
   30. *Lely's*] Sir Peter Lely, famous Dutch-English portrait painter.
   30. *truncheon*] officer's staff and badge of authority.

And look like heroes in a painted field;
But the coarse dauber of the coming scenes,
To follow life and nature only means;
Displays you as you are: makes his fine woman
A mercenary jilt, and true to no man;   35
His men of wit and pleasure of the age,
Are as dull rogues as ever cumbered stage:
He draws a friend, only to custom just,
And makes him naturally break his trust.
I, only, act a part like none of you;   40
And yet, you'll say, it is a fool's part too:
An honest man, who, like you, never winks
At faults; but, unlike you, speaks what he thinks:
The only fool who ne'er found patron yet;
For truth is now a fault, as well as wit.   45
And where else, but on stages, do we see
Truth pleasing; or rewarded honesty?
Which our bold poet does this day in me.
If not to th' honest, be to th' prosp'rous kind:
Some friends at court let the Plain Dealer find.   50

33. nature] *Q 1–7*; nature's *Q 8*, *O.*

THE PERSONS

MANLY, of an honest, surly, nice humor, supposed first in the time of the Dutch War to have procured the command of a ship, out of honor, not interest, and choosing a sea life only to avoid the world	*Mr. Hart*
FREEMAN, Manly's lieutenant, a gentleman well educated, but of a broken fortune, a complier with the age	*Mr. Kynaston*
VERNISH, Manly's bosom and only friend	*Mr. Griffin*
NOVEL, a pert, railing coxcomb and an admirer of novelties, makes love to Olivia	*Mr. Clark*
MAJOR OLDFOX, an old impertinent fop, given to scribbling, makes love to the Widow Blackacre	*Mr. Cartwright*
MY LORD PLAUSIBLE, a ceremonious, supple, commending coxcomb, in love with Olivia	*Mr. Haines*
JERRY BLACKACRE, a true raw squire, under age and his mother's government, bred to the law	*Mr. Charlton*
OLIVIA, Manly's mistress	*Mrs. Marshall*
FIDELIA, in love with Manly, and followed him to sea in man's clothes	*Mrs. Boutell*
ELIZA, cousin to Olivia	*Mrs. Knep*
LETTICE, Olivia's woman	*Mrs. Knight*
THE WIDOW BLACKACRE, a petulant, litigious widow, always in law, and mother to Squire Jerry	*Mrs. Cory*

The line numbers in the right margin are: 5, 10, 15, 20, 25.

LAWYERS, KNIGHTS OF THE POST, BAYLIFFS, AN ALDERMAN, A BOOKSELLER'S PRENTICE, A FOOTBOY, SAILORS, WAITERS AND ATTENDANTS

The Scene: *London*

1. *Hart*] *Q 1–5, Q8, O*; Heart *Q6–7*.
6. *Kynaston*] *Q1–2*; Kynastan *Q 3–8, O*.
10. NOVEL] *Q 3–8, O*; Novell *Q 1–2*.
15. *Haines*] *Q1*; Hains *Q 2–8, O*.
19. *Marshall*] *Q 1–3*; Marshal *Q 4–8, O*.
23. LETTICE] *Q 2–8, O*; Letice *Q 1*.
27. AN ALDERMAN] *Q 1–2*; and alderman *Q 3*; and aldermen *Q 4–8, O*.

2. *Dutch War*] of 1664–1667 or, more likely, the recent one of 1672–1674.
27. *Knights of the Post*] professional false witnesses.

The Plain Dealer

ACT I

Captain Manly's lodging.
Enter Captain Manly, *surlily, and my* Lord Plausible *following him, and*
two Sailors *behind.*

MANLY.

Tell not me, my good Lord Plausible, of your decorums,
supercilious forms, and slavish ceremonies; your little tricks,
which you the spaniels of the world do daily over and over
for and to one another; not out of love or duty, but your
servile fear.   5

LORD PLAUSIBLE.

Nay, i'faith, i'faith, you are too passionate, and I must
humbly beg your pardon and leave to tell you, they are the
arts, and rules, the prudent of the world walk by.

MANLY.

Let them. But I'll have no leading-strings. I can walk alone.
I hate a harness, and will not tug on in a faction, kissing my   10
leader behind, that another slave may do the like to me.

LORD PLAUSIBLE.

What, will you be singular then, like nobody, follow, love,
and esteem nobody?

MANLY.

Rather than be general, like you, follow everybody, court
and kiss everybody, though perhaps at the same time you   15
hate everybody.

LORD PLAUSIBLE.

Why, seriously, with your pardon, my dear friend—

MANLY.

With your pardon, my no friend, I will not, as you do,
whisper my hatred or my scorn, call a man fool or knave by
signs or mouths over his shoulder whilst you have him in   20

your arms. For such as you, like common whores and pickpockets, are only dangerous to those you embrace.

LORD PLAUSIBLE.

Such as I! Heavens defend me—upon my honor—

MANLY.

Upon your title, my lord, if you'd have me believe you.

LORD PLAUSIBLE.

Well then, as I am a person of honor, I never attempted to   25
abuse, or lessen any person, in my life.

MANLY.

What, you were afraid?

LORD PLAUSIBLE.

No, but seriously, I hate to do a rude thing. No, faith, I
speak well of all mankind.

MANLY.

I thought so, but know that speaking well of all mankind is   30
the worst kind of detraction, for it takes away the reputation
of the few good men in the world by making all alike. Now
I speak ill of most men, because they deserve it, I that can
do a rude thing rather than an unjust thing.

LORD PLAUSIBLE.

Well, tell not me, my dear friend, what people deserve. I   35
ne'er mind that. I, like an author in a dedication, never
speak well of a man for his sake but my own. I will not disparage any man to disparage myself. For to speak ill of
people behind their backs is not like a person of honor, and
truly to speak ill of them to their faces is not like a com-   40
plaisant person. But if I did say or do an ill thing to anybody, it should be sure to be behind their backs out of pure
good manners.

MANLY.

Very well, but I, that am an unmannerly sea fellow, if I ever
speak well of people (which is very seldom indeed), it   45
should be sure to be behind their backs, and if I would say
or do ill to any, it should be to their faces. I would justle a
proud, strutting, overlooking coxcomb at the head of his
sycophants rather than put out my tongue at him when he
were past me, would frown in the arrogant, big, dull face of   50

41–42. anybody] *Q1*; any *Q2–8, O.*

---

an overgrown knave of business, rather than vent my spleen against him when his back were turned, would give fawning slaves the lie whilst they embrace or commend me, cowards whilst they brag; call a rascal by no other title, though his father had left him a duke's, laugh at fools aloud 55 before their mistresses, and must desire people to leave me when their visits grow at last as troublesome as they were at first impertinent.

LORD PLAUSIBLE.

I would not have my visits troublesome.

MANLY.

The only way to be sure not to have them troublesome is to 60 make them when people are not at home. For your visits, like other good turns, are most obliging when made or done to a man in his absence. A pox, why should anyone, because he has nothing to do, go and disturb another man's business? 65

LORD PLAUSIBLE.

I beg your pardon, my dear friend. What, you have business?

MANLY.

If you have any, I would not detain your lordship.

LORD PLAUSIBLE.

Detain me, dear sir! I can never have enough of your company. 70

MANLY.

I'm afraid I should be tiresome. I know not what you think.

LORD PLAUSIBLE.

Well, dear sir, I see you would have me gone.

MANLY (aside).

But I see you won't.

LORD PLAUSIBLE.

Your most faithful—

MANLY.

God be w'ye, my lord. 75

LORD PLAUSIBLE.

Your most humble—

MANLY.

Farewell.

LORD PLAUSIBLE.

> And eternally—

MANLY.

> And eternally ceremony— (*Aside.*) Then the devil take
> thee eternally.   80

LORD PLAUSIBLE.

> You shall use no ceremony, by my life.

MANLY.

> I do not intend it.

LORD PLAUSIBLE.

> Why do you stir then?

MANLY.

> Only to see you out of doors, that I may shut them against
> more welcomes.   85

LORD PLAUSIBLE.

> Nay, faith, that shan't pass upon your most faithful, humble
> servant.

MANLY (*aside*).

> Nor this any more upon me.

LORD PLAUSIBLE.

> Well, you are too strong for me.

MANLY (*aside*).

> I'd sooner be visited by the plague, for that only would keep   90
> a man from visits and his doors shut.

> > *Exit, thrusting out my* Lord Plausible. *Manent* Sailors.

1 SAILOR.

> Here's a finical fellow, Jack! What a brave fair-weather
> captain of a ship he would make!

2 SAILOR.

> He a captain of a ship! It must be when she's in the dock
> then, for he looks like one of those that get the king's com-   95
> missions for hulls to sell a king's ship, when a brave fellow
> has fought her almost to a longboat.

1 SAILOR.

> On my conscience then, Jack, that's the reason our bully
> tar sunk our ship: not only that the Dutch might not have
> her, but that the courtiers, who laugh at wooden legs, might   100
> not make her prize.

2 SAILOR.

> A pox of his sinking, Tom; we have made a base, broken,
> short voyage of it.

1 SAILOR.

Ay, your brisk dealers in honor always make quick returns
with their ship to the dock and their men to the hospitals. 105
'Tis, let me see, just a month since we set out of the river,
and the wind was almost as cross to us as the Dutch.

2 SAILOR.

Well, I forgive him sinking my own poor truck, if he
would but have given me time and leave to have saved
black Kate of Wapping's small venture. 110

1 SAILOR.

Faith, I forgive him since, as the purser told me, he sunk
the value of five or six thousand pounds of his own with
which he was to settle himself somewhere in the Indies,
for our merry lieutenant was to succeed him in his com-
mission for the ship back, for he was resolved never to 115
return again for England.

2 SAILOR.

So it seemed by his fighting.

1 SAILOR.

No, but he was a-weary of this side of the world here, they
say.

2 SAILOR.

Ay, or else he would not have bid so fair for a passage into 120
t'other.

1 SAILOR.

Jack, thou think'st thyself in the forecastle, thou'rt so
waggish; but I tell you then, he had a mind to go live and
bask himself on the sunny side of the globe.

2 SAILOR.

What, out of any discontent? For he's always as dogged as 125
an old tarpaulin when hindered of a voyage by a young
pantaloon captain.

1 SAILOR.

'Tis true, I never saw him pleased but in the fight, and then
he looked like one of us coming from the pay table, with a
new lining to our hats under our arms. 130

108. truck] *Q1–3*; trunck *Q4–5*;   129. pay table] *Q1–2*, *Q4–8*, *O*;
trunk *Q6–8*, *O*.   play-table *Q3*.

---

110. *Wapping*] Thames-side suburb below the Tower.
127. *pantaloon*] breeches fashionable with the young men of the day.

2 SAILOR.

A pox, he's like the Bay of Biscay, rough and angry, let the
wind blow where 'twill.

1 SAILOR.

Nay, there's no more dealing with him than with the land
in a storm, no-near—

2 SAILOR.

'Tis a hurry-durry blade. Dost thou remember after we 135
had tugged hard the old leaky longboat to save his life,
when I welcomed him ashore, he gave me a box on the
ear and called me fawning water dog?

Enter Manly *and* Freeman.

1 SAILOR.

Hold thy peace, Jack, and stand by, the foul weather's
coming.   140

MANLY.

You rascals, dogs, how could this tame thing get through
you?

1 SAILOR.

Faith, to tell your honor the truth, we were at hob in the
hall, and whilst my brother and I were quarreling about
a cast, he slunk by us.   145

2 SAILOR.

He's a sneaking fellow I warrant for it.

MANLY.

Have more care for the future, you slaves. Go and with
drawn cutlasses stand at the stair foot and keep all that ask
for me from coming up. Suppose you were guarding the
scuttle to the powder room. Let none enter here at your 150
and their peril.

1 SAILOR.

No, for the danger would be the same; you would blow
them and us up if we should.

2 SAILOR.

Must no one come to you, sir?

141. rascals] *Q 1–2, O*; rascal *Q 3–8.*   151. and] *Q 1–3, O*; or *Q 4–8.*

135. *hurry-durry*] roughly impetuous.
143. *hob*] a coin-tossing game.

MANLY.

No man, sir.   155

1 SAILOR.

No man, sir, but a woman then, an't like your honor—

MANLY.

No woman neither, you impertinent dog. Would you be
pimping? A sea pimp is the strangest monster she has.

2 SAILOR.

Indeed, an't like your honor, 'twill be hard for us to deny a
woman anything since we are so newly come on shore.   160

1 SAILOR.

We'll let no old woman come up, though it were our trusting
landlady at Wapping.

MANLY.

Would you be witty, you brandy casks you? You become
a jest as ill as you do a horse. Be gone, you dogs, I hear a
noise on the stairs.   *Exeunt* Sailors. 165

FREEMAN.

Faith, I am sorry you would let the fop go. I intended to
have had some sport with him.

MANLY.

Sport with him! A pox! Then why did you not stay? You
should have enjoyed your coxcomb and had him to yourself
for me.   170

FREEMAN.

No, I should not have cared for him without you neither.
For the pleasure which fops afford is like that of drinking,
only good when 'tis shared; and a fool, like a bottle, which
would make you merry in company, will make you dull
alone. But how the devil could you turn a man of his quality 175
down stairs? You use a lord with very little ceremony, it
seems.

MANLY.

A lord! What, thou art one of those who esteem men only
by the marks and value fortune has set upon them, and
never consider intrinsic worth. But counterfeit honor will 180
not be current with me. I weigh the man, not his title. 'Tis

163. casks] *Q1–5, Q8, O*; cask
Q6–7.

not the king's stamp can make the metal better or heavier.
Your lord is a leaden shilling, which you may bend every
way; and debases the stamp he bears, instead of being raised
by it. —Here again, you slaves?   185

Enter Sailors.

1 SAILOR.

Only to receive farther instructions, an't like your honor.
What if a man should bring you money? Should we turn
him back?

MANLY.

All men, I say. Must I be pestered with you too? You dogs,
away.   190

2 SAILOR.

Nay, I know one man your honor would not have us hinder
coming to you, I'm sure.

MANLY.

Who's that? Speak quickly, slaves.

2 SAILOR.

Why, a man that should bring you a challenge, for though
you refuse money, I'm sure you love fighting too well to 195
refuse that.

MANLY.

Rogue, rascal, dog.

Kicks the Sailors *out.*

FREEMAN.

Nay, let the poor rogues have their forecastle jests. They
cannot help them in a fight, scarce when a ship's sinking.

MANLY.

Damn their untimely jests. A servant's jest is more sauciness 200
than his counsel.

FREEMAN.

But what, will you see nobody? Not your friends?

MANLY.

Friends—I have but one, and he, I hear, is not in town.
Nay, can have but one friend, for a true heart admits but of
one friendship as of one love. But in having that friend I 205
have a thousand, for he has the courage of men in despair,
yet the diffidency and caution of cowards, the secrecy of the
revengeful and the constancy of martyrs, one fit to advise, to
keep a secret, to fight and die for his friend. Such I think
him, for I have trusted him with my mistress in my absence, 210

and the trust of beauty is sure the greatest we can show.

FREEMAN.

Well, but all your good thoughts are not for him alone, I
hope. Pray, what do you think of me for a friend?

MANLY.

Of thee! Why, thou are a latitudinarian in friendship, that
is, no friend. Thou dost side with all mankind but will 215
suffer for none. Thou are indeed like your Lord Plausible,
the pink of courtesy, therefore hast no friendship. For
ceremony and great professing renders friendship as much
suspected as it does religion.

FREEMAN.

And no professing, no ceremony at all in friendship, were 220
as unnatural and as undecent as in religion. And there is
hardly such a thing as an honest hypocrite, who professes
himself to be worse than he is, unless it be yourself. For
though I could never get you to say you were my friend, I
know you'll prove so.   225

MANLY.

I must confess I am so much your friend I would not deceive
you, therefore must tell you, not only because my heart is
taken up but according to your rules of friendship, I cannot
be your friend.

FREEMAN.

Why, pray?   230

MANLY.

Because he that is, you'll say, a true friend to a man is a
friend to all his friends. But you must pardon me. I cannot
wish well to pimps, flatterers, detractors, and cowards, stiff
nodding knaves, and supple, pliant, kissing fools. Now, all
these I have seen you use like the dearest friends in the 235
world.

FREEMAN.

Hah, hah, hah— What, you observed me, I warrant, in the
galleries at Whitehall doing the business of the place!
Pshaw! Court professions, like court promises, go for nothing,
man. But, faith, could you think I was a friend to all those I 240
hugged, kissed, flattered, bowed to? Hah, ha—

241. bowed to] *Q3–8*; bowed too
Q1–2, O.

MANLY.

You told them so, and swore it too. I heard you.

FREEMAN.

Ay, but when their backs were turned did I not tell you they were rogues, villains, rascals whom I despised and hated?

MANLY.

Very fine! But what reason had I to believe you spoke your 245 heart to me since you professed deceiving so many?

FREEMAN.

Why, don't you know, good captain, that telling truth is a quality as prejudicial to a man that would thrive in the world as square play to a cheat, or true love to a whore! Would you have a man speak truth to his ruin? You are 250 severer than the law, which requires no man to swear against himself. You would have me speak truth against myself, I warrant, and tell my promising friend, the courtier, he has a bad memory?

MANLY.

Yes. 255

FREEMAN.

And so make him remember to forget my business. And I should tell the great lawyer too that he takes oftener fees to hold his tongue than to speak?

MANLY.

No doubt on't.

FREEMAN.

Ay, and have him hang or ruin me, when he should come 260 to be a judge and I before him. And you would have me tell the new officer who bought his employment lately that he is a coward?

MANLY.

Ay.

FREEMAN.

And so get myself cashiered, not him, he having the better 265 friends though I the better sword. And I should tell the scribbler of honor that heraldry were a prettier and fitter study for so fine a gentleman than poetry?

MANLY.

Certainly.

FREEMAN.

And so find myself mauled in his next hired lampoon. And 270

you would have me tell the holy lady too she lies with her
chaplain.

MANLY.

No doubt on't.

FREEMAN.

And so draw the clergy upon my back and want a good
table to dine at sometimes. And by the same reason too, 275
I should tell you that the world thinks you a madman, a
brutal, and have you cut my throat, or worse, hate me!
What other good success of all my plain dealing could I
have than what I've mentioned?

MANLY.

Why, first your promising courtier would keep his word, out 280
of fear of more reproaches; or at least would give you no
more vain hopes. Your lawyer would serve you more faithfully, for he, having no honor but his interest, is truest still
to him he knows suspects him. The new officer would provoke thee to make him a coward and so be cashiered, that 285
thou or some other honest fellow, who had more courage
than money, might get his place. The noble sonneteer would
trouble thee no more with his madrigals. The praying lady
would leave off railing at wenching before thee and not turn
away her chambermaid for her own known frailty with thee. 290
And I, instead of hating thee, should love thee for thy plain
dealing, and in lieu of being mortified am proud that the
world and I think not well of one another.

FREEMAN.

Well, doctors differ. You are for plain dealing, I find. But
against your particular notions I have the practice of the 295
whole world. Observe but any morning what people do
when they get together on the Exchange, in Westminster
Hall, or the galleries in Whitehall.

MANLY.

I must confess, there they seem to rehearse Bays's grand
dance: here you see a bishop bowing low to a gaudy atheist, 300
a judge to a doorkeeper, a great lord to a fishmonger or a

297–298. *Exchange, Westminster Hall, Whitehall*] examples of "the whole
world": merchants, lawyers, courtiers.
299–300. *Bays's grand dance*] an absurd dance in *The Rehearsal*, 1671.

scrivener with a jack-chain about his neck, a lawyer to
a sergeant at arms, a velvet physician to a threadbare
chemist, and a supple gentleman usher to a surly beefeater,
and so tread 'round in a preposterous huddle of ceremony   305
to each other, whilst they can hardly hold their solemn
false countenances.

FREEMAN.

Well, they understand the world.

MANLY.

Which I do not, I confess.

FREEMAN.

But, sir, pray believe the friendship I promise you real,   310
whatsoever I have professed to others. Try me at least.

MANLY.

Why, what would you do for me?

FREEMAN.

I would fight for you.

MANLY.

That you would do for your own honor. But what else?

FREEMAN.

I would lend you money, if I had it.   315

MANLY.

To borrow more of me another time. That were but putting
your money to interest. A usurer would be as good a friend.
But what other piece of friendship?

FREEMAN.

I would speak well of you to your enemies.

MANLY.

To encourage others to be your friends by a show of grati-   320
tude. But what else?

FREEMAN.

Nay, I would not hear you ill spoken of behind your back
by my friend.

MANLY.

Nay, then thou'rt a friend indeed. But it were unreasonable
to expect it from thee as the world goes now, when new   325

316. but] *Q 1–6, Q 8, O; om. Q 7.*

---

302. *scrivener . . . neck*] a notary wearing his badge of office.

friends, like new mistresses, are got by disparaging old ones.

Enter Fidelia.

But here comes another will say as much at least. Dost not
thou love me devilishly too, my little volunteer, as well as
he or any man can?

FIDELIA.

Better than any man can love you, my dear captain.   330

MANLY.

Look you there. I told you so.

FIDELIA.

As well as you do truth or honor, sir, as well.

MANLY.

Nay, good young gentleman, enough, for shame. Thou hast
been a page, by thy flattering and lying, to one of those
praying ladies who love flattery so well they are jealous of it, 335
and wert turned away for saying the same things to the old
housekeeper for sweetmeats as you did to your lady. For
thou flatterest everything and everybody alike.

FIDELIA.

You, dear sir, should not suspect the truth of what I say of
you, though to you. Fame, the old liar, is believed when she 340
speaks wonders of you. You cannot be flattered, sir. Your
merit is unspeakable.

MANLY.

Hold, hold, sir, or I shall suspect worse of you, that you have
been a cushion-bearer to some state hypocrite and turned
away by the chaplains for out-flattering their probation 345
sermons for a benefice.

FIDELIA.

Suspect me for anything, sir, but the want of love, faith, and
duty to you, the bravest, worthiest of mankind. Believe me,
I could die for you, sir.

MANLY.

Nay, there you lie, sir. Did I not see thee more afraid in the 350
fight than the chaplain of the ship or the purser that bought
his place?

327–328. not thou] *Q1–7*; thou not   340. she] *Q1–6, Q8, O*; he *Q7.*
Q8, O.   350. I not] *Q1–7*; not I *Q8, O.*

FIDELIA.

Can he be said to be afraid that ventures to sea with you?

MANLY.

Fie, fie, no more. I shall hate thy flattery worse than thy
cowardice, nay, than thy bragging.   355

FIDELIA.

Well, I own then I was afraid, mightily afraid. Yet for you
I would be afraid again, an hundred times afraid. Dying is
ceasing to be afraid, and that I could do sure for you and
you'll believe me one day.   *Weeps.*

FREEMAN.

Poor youth! Believe his eyes if not his tongue. He seems to 360
speak truth with them.

MANLY.

What, does he cry? A pox on't, a maudlin flatterer is as
nauseously troublesome as a maudlin drunkard. No more,
you little milksop. Do not cry. I'll never make thee afraid
again, for of all men, if I had occasion, thou shouldst not be 365
my second. And when I go to sea again, thou shalt venture
thy life no more with me.

FIDELIA.

Why, will you leave me behind then? (*Aside.*) If you
would preserve my life, I'm sure you should not.

MANLY.

Leave thee behind! Ay, ay, thou art a hopeful youth for the 370
shore only. Here thou wilt live to be cherished by fortune
and the great ones. For thou may'st easily come to out-
flatter a dull poet, out-lie a coffeehouse or gazette writer,
out-swear a knight of the post, out-watch a pimp, out-fawn
a rook, out-promise a lover, out-rail a wit, and out-brag a 375
sea-captain. All this thou canst do, because thou'rt a coward,
a thing I hate. Therefore thou'lt do better with the world
than with me, and these are the good courses you must take
in the world. There's good advice, at least, at parting. Go
and be happy with it.   380

FIDELIA.

Parting, sir! O let me not hear that dismal word.

354. shall] *Q1–7, O; om. Q8.*   365. of] *Q1–2, Q5–8, O; om. Q3–4.*

MANLY.

If my words frighten thee, be gone the sooner; for, to be
plain with thee, cowardice and I cannot dwell together.

FIDELIA.

And cruelty and courage never dwelt together sure, sir. Do
not turn me off to shame and misery, for I am helpless and 385
friendless.

MANLY.

Friendless! There are half a score friends for thee then.
(*Offers her gold.*) I leave myself no more. They'll help thee
a little. Be gone! Go! I must be cruel to thee (if thou call'st
it so) out of pity. 390

FIDELIA.

If you would be cruelly pitiful, sir, let it be with your sword,
not gold. *Exit.*

Enter First Sailor.

1 SAILOR.

We have with much ado turned away two gentlemen who
told us forty times over their names were Mr. Novel and
Major Oldfox. 395

MANLY.

Well, to your post again. *Exit* Sailor.
But how come those puppies coupled always together?

FREEMAN.

O, the coxcombs keep each other company to show each
other, as Novel calls it, or, as Oldfox says, like two knives
to whet one another. 400

MANLY.

And set other people's teeth an edge.

Enter Second Sailor.

2 SAILOR.

Here is a woman, an't like your honor, scolds and bustles
with us to come in, as much as a seaman's widow at the
Navy Office. Her name is Mrs. Blackacre.

383. cowardice] *Q1–6, Q8, O;*   *Q2–8.*
cowardness *Q7.*   399. knives] *Q1–6, Q8, O;* knaves
391. sword] *Q1, O;* sword, and   *Q7.*

MANLY.

That fiend too! 405

FREEMAN.

The Widow Blackacre, is it not? That litigious she-petty-fogger, who is at law and difference with all the world; but I wish I could make her agree with me in the church. They say she has fifteen hundred pounds a year jointure and the care of her son, that is, the destruction of his estate. 410

MANLY.

Her lawyers, attorneys and solicitors have fifteen hundred pound a year whilst she is contented to be poor to make other people so, for she is as vexatious as her father was, the great attorney, nay, as a dozen Norfolk attorneys, and as implacable an adversary as a wife suing for alimony or a 415 parson for his tithes; and she loves an Easter term, or any term, not as other country ladies do, to come up to be fine, cuckold their husbands, and take their pleasure. For she has no pleasure but in vexing others and is usually clothed and daggled like a bawd in disguise, pursued through alleys 420 by sergeants. When she is in town she lodges in one of the Inns of Chancery, where she breeds her son and is herself his tutoress in law French. And for her country abode, though she has no estate there, she chooses Norfolk. But bid her come in with a pox to her. She is Olivia's kinswoman 425 and may make me amends for her visit by some discourse of that dear woman. *Exit* Sailor.

Enter Widow Blackacre *with a mantle and a green bag and several papers in the other hand,* Jerry Blackacre *her son, in a gown, laden with green bags, following her.*

WIDOW.

I never had so much to do with a judge's doorkeeper, as with yours, but—

---

416. *Easter term*] The English courts divided the year into four terms: Hilary, Easter, Trinity, and Michaelmas.
420. *daggled*] muddy, spattered—modern "draggled" or "bedraggled."
422. *Inns of Chancery*] residence of law students.
424. *Norfolk*] The people of Norfolk were notoriously litigious.
427.2. *green bags*] contemporary badge of the law student or lawyer.

MANLY.

But the incomparable Olivia, how does she since I went?   430

WIDOW.

Since you went, my suit—

MANLY.

Olivia, I say, is she well?

WIDOW.

My suit, if you had not returned—

MANLY.

Damn your suit. How does your cousin Olivia?

WIDOW.

My suit, I say, had been quite lost, but now—   435

MANLY.

But now, where is Olivia? In town? For—

WIDOW.

For tomorrow we are to have a hearing.

MANLY.

Would you'd let me have a hearing today.

WIDOW.

But why won't you hear me?

MANLY.

I am no judge and you talk of nothing but suits. But, pray 440
tell me, when did you see Olivia?

WIDOW.

I am no visitor but a woman of business, or if I ever visit
'tis only the Chancery Lane ladies, ladies towards the law
and not any of your lazy, good-for-nothing flirts, who cannot read law French, though a gallant writ it. But, as I was 445
telling you, my suit—

MANLY.

Damn these impertinent, vexatious people of business, of all
sexes. They are still troubling the world with the tedious
recitals of their lawsuits, and one can no more stop their
mouths than a wit's when he talks of himself, or an intelli- 450
gencer's when he talks of other people.

WIDOW.

And a pox of all vexatious, impertinent lovers. They are

438. Would you'd] *Q1–7*; Wou'd
you wou'd *Q8, O.*

still perplexing the world with the tedious narrations of
their love-suits and discourses of their mistresses. You are as
troublesome to a poor widow of business as a young cox- 455
combly rithming lover.

MANLY.

And thou art as troublesome to me as a rook to a losing
gamester or a young putter of cases to his mistress and
sempstress, who has love in her head for another.

WIDOW.

Nay, since you talk of putting of cases and will not hear me 460
speak, hear our Jerry a little. Let him put our case to you, for
the trial's tomorrow, and since you are my chief witness, I
would have your memory refreshed and your judgment
informed, that you may not give your evidence improperly.
Speak out, child.   465

JERRY.

Yes, forsooth. Hemh! Hemh! John-a-Stiles—

MANLY.

You may talk, young lawyer, but I shall no more mind you
than a hungry judge does a cause after the clock has struck
one.

FREEMAN.

Nay, you'll find him as peevish too.   470

WIDOW.

No matter. Jerry, go on. Do you observe it then, sir, for I
think I have seen you in a gown once. Lord, I could hear
our Jerry put cases all day long! Mark him, sir.

JERRY.

John-a-Stiles—no— There are first Fitz, Pere, and Ayle—
No, no, Ayle, Pere, and Fitz. Ayle is seized in fee of Black- 475
acre; John-a-Stiles disseizes Ayle; Ayle makes claim, and
the disseizor dies; then the Ayle—no, the Fitz.

WIDOW.

No, the Pere, sirrah.

455–456. coxcombly] *Q 1–2, O*; coxcomb *Q 3–8*.

456. rithming] *Q 1–3*; riming *Q 4–7*;
rhiming *Q 8, O*.
458. and] *Q 1–7*; or *Q 8, O*.

466. *John-a-Stiles*] English cousin in law jargon to John Doe and Richard
Roe, just as *Ayle, Pere*, and *Fitz* (l. 475) are French cousins.

JERRY.

O, the Pere. Ay, the Pere, sir, and the Fitz—no, the Ayle;
no, the Pere and the Fitz, sir, and—   480

MANLY.

Damn Pere, Mere, and Fitz, sir.

WIDOW.

No, you are out, child. Hear me, captain, then. There are
Ayle, Pere, and Fitz. Ayle is seized in fee of Blackacre and
being so seized, John-a-Stiles disseizes the Ayle, Ayle makes
claim, and the disseizer dies. And then the Pere re-enters, 485
the Pere sirrah, the Pere—(*To* Jerry.)   And the Fitz enters
upon the Pere, and the Ayle brings his writ of disseizin in
the *post*, and the Pere brings his writ of disseizin in the *per*
and—

MANLY.

Can'st thou hear this stuff, Freeman? I could as soon suffer 490
a whole noise of flatterers at a great man's levy in a morning.
But thou hast servile complacency enough to listen to a
quibbling statesman in disgrace, nay, and be beforehand
with him in laughing at his dull no-jest. But I—

                              Offering to go out.

WIDOW.

Nay, sir, hold. Where's the subpoena, Jerry? I must serve 495
you, sir. You are required by this to give your testimony—

MANLY.

I'll be forsworn to be revenged on thee.

                    Exit Manly, *throwing away the subpoena.*

WIDOW.

Get you gone for a lawless companion. Come, Jerry. I had
almost forgot we were to meet at the master's at three. Let
us mind our business still, child.   500

JERRY.

I, forsooth, e'en so let's.

488. *per*] *Q2*; *pere Q1, Q3–8, O.*   491. in a] *Q1–3, O*; in the *Q4–8.*

482–489. *No . . . per and*—] The case recited involves a complex suit and
countersuit over alleged dispossession. The *per*, of *post* and *per*, which has to
do with the manner in which the action is brought, has caused some
trouble to printers, who confuse it with *Pere*, one of the parties to the suit.

FREEMAN.

Nay, madam, now I would beg you to hear me a little, a little of my business.

WIDOW.

I have business of my own calls me away, sir.

FREEMAN.

My business would prove yours too, dear madam.   505

WIDOW.

Yours would be some sweet business, I warrant. What, 'tis no Westminster Hall business? Would you have my advice?

FREEMAN.

No, faith, 'tis a little Westminster Abbey business. I would have your consent.

WIDOW.

O fie, fie, sir, to me such discourse before my dear minor 510 there!

JERRY.

Ay, ay, Mother, he would be taking livery and seizin of your jointure by digging the turf, but I'll watch your waters, bully, ifac. Come away, Mother.

Exit Jerry, *haling away his* Mother.

Manet Freeman. *Enter to him* Fidelia.

FIDELIA.

Dear sir, you have pity. Beget but some in our captain for 515 me.

FREEMAN.

Where is he?

FIDELIA.

Within, swearing as much as he did in the great storm and cursing you and sometimes sinks into calms and sighs and talks of his Olivia.   520

FREEMAN.

He would never trust me to see her. Is she handsome?

514.1. *haling*] *Q1*; hailing *Q2–7*;   515. our] *Q1–3, O*; your *Q4–8*. hauling *Q8, O*.

512. *livery and seizin*] more law-French, this phrase meaning delivery of corporal possession, symbolized by the bit of turf.
514. *ifac*] dialectal form of "in faith."

FIDELIA.

No, if you'll take my word, but I am not a proper judge.

FREEMAN.

What is she?

FIDELIA.

A gentlewoman, I suppose, but of as mean a fortune as beauty, but her relations would not suffer her to go with 525 him to the Indies, and his aversion to this side of the world, together with the late opportunity of commanding the convoy, would not let him stay here longer, though to enjoy her.

FREEMAN.

He loves her mightily then. 530

FIDELIA.

Yes, so well that the remainder of his fortune (I hear about five or six thousand pounds) he has left her in case he had died by the way or before she could prevail with her friends to follow him, which he expected she should do, and has left behind him his great bosom friend to be her convoy to him. 535

FREEMAN.

What charms has she for him if she be not handsome?

FIDELIA.

He fancies her, I suppose, the only woman of truth and sincerity in the world.

FREEMAN.

No common beauty I confess.

FIDELIA.

Or else sure he would not have trusted her with so great a 540 share of his fortune in his absence, I suppose (since his late loss) all he has.

FREEMAN.

Why, has he left it in her own custody?

FIDELIA.

I am told so.

FREEMAN.

Then he has showed love to her indeed in leaving her, like 545 an old husband that dies as soon as he has made his wife a

---

525. relations] *Q1–6, Q8, O*; relation *Q7.*

525–526. with him to] *Q1, Q3–8, O*; to with him *Q2.*

good jointure. But I'll go in to him and speak for you and
know more from him of his Olivia.   *Exit. Manet* Fidelia *sola.*

FIDELIA.

His Olivia indeed, his happy Olivia,
Yet she was left behind, when I was with him.   550
But she was ne'er out of his mind or heart.
She has told him she loved him; I have showed it.
And durst not tell him so till I had done,
Under this habit, such convincing acts
Of loving friendship for him that through it   555
He first might find out both my sex and love.
And, when I'd had him from his fair Olivia
And this bright world of artful beauties here,
Might then have hoped he would have looked on me
Amongst the sooty Indians. And I could   560
To choose there live his wife, where wives are forced
To live no longer when their husbands die.
Nay, what's yet worse, to share them whil'st they live
With many rival wives. But here he comes,
And I must yet keep out of his sight, not   565
To lose it forever.   *Exit.*

Enter Manly *and* Freeman.

FREEMAN.

But, pray, what strange charms has she that could make you
love?

MANLY.

Strange charms indeed! She has beauty enough to call in
question her wit or virtue, and her form would make a   570
starved hermit a ravisher; yet her virtue and conduct would
preserve her from the subtle lust of a pampered prelate. She
is so perfect a beauty that art could not better it nor affectation deform it; yet all this is nothing. Her tongue, as well as
face, ne'er knew artifice; nor ever did her words or looks con-   575
tradict her heart. She is all truth and hates the lying, mask-
ing, daubing world as I do. For which I love her and for
which I think she dislikes not me. For she has often shut out

557. had] *Q 1-3, O*; have *Q 4-8*.   affection *Q 3-8*.
573-574. affectation] *Q 1-2, O*;   575. ever] *Q 1-7, O*; never *Q 8*.

of her conversation for mine the gaudy, fluttering parrots of
the town, apes and echoes of men only, and refused their 580
commonplace pert chat, flattery, and submissions, to be
entertained with my sullen bluntness and honest love. And,
last of all swore to me since her parents would not suffer her
to go with me, she would stay behind for no other man, but
follow me without their leave, if not to be obtained. Which 585
oath—

FREEMAN.

Did you think she would keep?

MANLY.

Yes, for she is not (I tell you) like other women, but can
keep her promise, though she has sworn to keep it. But that
she might the better keep it I left her the value of five or six 590
thousand pound. For women's wants are generally their
most importunate solicitors to love or marriage.

FREEMAN.

And money summons lovers more than beauty, and aug-
ments but their importunity and their number, so makes it
the harder for a woman to deny them. For my part, I am 595
for the French maxim: if you would have your female subjects loyal, keep them poor. But, in short, that your mistress
may not marry, you have given her a portion.

MANLY.

She had given me her heart first and I am satisfied with the
security. I can never doubt her truth and constancy. 600

FREEMAN.

It seems you do since you are fain to bribe it with money.
But how come you to be so diffident of the man that says he
loves you and not doubt the woman that says it?

MANLY.

I should, I confess, doubt the love of any other woman but
her, as I do the friendship of any other man but him I have 605
trusted, but I have such proofs of their faith as cannot deceive
me.

FREEMAN.

Cannot!

591. pound] *Q1–2*; pounds *Q3–8*,
O.

MANLY.

Not but I know that generally no man can be a great enemy
but under the name of friend. And if you are a cuckold, it 610
is your friend only that makes you so, for your enemy is not
admitted to your house. If you are cheated in your fortune,
'tis your friend that does it, for your enemy is not made your
trustee. If your honor or good name be injured, 'tis your
friend that does it still, because your enemy is not believed 615
against you. Therefore I rather choose to go where honest,
downright barbarity is professed, where men devour one
another like generous hungry lions and tigers, not like croco-
diles, where they think the devil white, of our complexion,
and I am already so far an Indian. But if your weak faith 620
doubts this miracle of a woman, come along with me and
believe and thou wilt find her so handsome that thou, who
art so much my friend, wilt have a mind to lie with her and
so will not fail to discover what her faith and thine is to me.

When we're in love, the great adversity,   625
Our friends and mistresses at once we try.

Finis actus primi

624. will] *Q 1–4, Q 8, O*; wilt *Q 5–7.*

ACT II

Olivia's Lodging.
Enter Olivia, Eliza, Lettice.

OLIVIA.
　Ah, cousin, what a world 'tis we live in! I am so weary of it.

ELIZA.
　Truly, cousin, I can find no fault with it but that we cannot
　always live in it. For I can never be weary of it.

OLIVIA.
　O hideous! You cannot be in earnest sure when you say you
　like the filthy world.　　　　　　　　　　　　　　　　　5

ELIZA.
　You cannot be in earnest sure when you say you dislike it.

OLIVIA.
　You are a very censorious creature, I find.

ELIZA.
　I must confess I think we women as often discover where
　we love by railing, as men when they lie by their swearing,
　and the world is but a constant keeping gallant, whom we　10
　fail not to quarrel with when anything crosses us yet cannot
　part with it for our hearts.

LETTICE.
　A gallant indeed, madam, whom ladies first make jealous
　and then quarrel with it for being so. For if, by her indis-
　cretion, a lady be talked of for a man, she cries presently,　15
　"'Tis a censorious world." If by her vanity the intrigue be
　found out, "'Tis a prying, malicious world." If by her over-
　fondness the gallant proves unconstant, "'Tis a false world."
　And if by her niggardliness the chambermaid tells, "'Tis a
　perfidious world." But that I'm sure your ladyship cannot　20
　say of the world yet, as bad as 'tis.

OLIVIA.
　But I may say, "'Tis a very impertinent world." Hold your
　peace. And, cousin, if the world be a gallant, 'tis such an
　one as is my aversion. Pray name it no more.

14–15. indiscretion] *Q1–4, Q8, O;*　　17. If by] *Q1–2;* And if *Q3–8, O.*
discretion *Q5–7.*

－37－

ELIZA.

But is it possible the world, which has such variety of   25
charms for other women, can have none for you? Let's see—
first, what d'ye think of dressing and fine clothing?

OLIVIA.

Dressing! Fie, fie, 'tis my aversion. But come hither, you
dowdy, methinks you might have opened this toure better.
O hideous! I cannot suffer it! D'ye see how't sits?   30

ELIZA.

Well enough, cousin, if dressing be your aversion.

OLIVIA.

'Tis so, and for variety of rich clothes, they are more my
aversion.

LETTICE.

Ay, 'tis because your ladyship wears them too long, for
indeed a gown, like a gallant, grows one's aversion by having   35
too much of it.

OLIVIA.

Insatiable creature! I'll be sworn I have had this not above
three days, cousin, and within this month have made some
six more.

ELIZA.

Then your aversion to them is not altogether so great.   40

OLIVIA.

Alas! 'Tis for my woman only I wear them, cousin.

LETTICE.

If it be for me only, madam, pray do not wear them.

ELIZA.

But what d'ye think of visits—balls—

OLIVIA.

O, I detest them.

ELIZA.

Of plays?   45

OLIVIA.

I abominate them: filthy, obscene, hideous things.

ELIZA.

What say you to masquerading in the winter and Hyde
Park in the summer?

42. be] *Q1–6, Q8, O*; be but *Q7*.

---

29. *toure*] a false hairpiece.

OLIVIA.
Insipid pleasures I taste not.

ELIZA.
Nay, if you are for more solid pleasure, what think you of a   50
rich, young husband?

OLIVIA.
O horrid! Marriage! What a pleasure you have found out!
I nauseate it of all things.

LETTICE.
But what does your ladyship think then of a liberal, handsome young lover?   55

OLIVIA.
A handsome young fellow, you impudent! Be gone, out of
my sight. Name a handsome young fellow to me! Foh, a
hideous, handsome young fellow I abominate.   *Spits.*

ELIZA.
Indeed! But let's see—will nothing please you? What d'ye
think of the court?   60

OLIVIA.
How, the court? The court, cousin, my aversion, my aversion, my aversion of all aversions.

ELIZA.
How? The court! Where—

OLIVIA.
Where sincerity is a quality as out of fashion and as un-
prosperous as bashfulness. I could not laugh at a quibble,   65
though it were a fat privy counselor's, nor praise a lord's ill
verses, though I were myself the subject, nor an old lady's
young looks, though I were her woman; nor sit to a vain
young simile-maker, though he flattered me. In short, I
could not gloat upon a man when he comes into a room and   70
laugh at him when he goes out. I cannot rail at the absent
to flatter the standers-by. I—

ELIZA.
Well, but railing now is so common that 'tis no more malice
but the fashion, and the absent think they are no more the
worse for being railed at than the present think they are the   75
better for being flattered. And for the court—

50. pleasure] Q1-2, O; pleasures   69. simile-maker]   Q1-8; smile-
Q3-8.   maker O.

OLIVIA.

Nay, do not defend the court, for you'll make me rail at it, like a trusting citizen's widow.

ELIZA.

Or like a Holborn lady, who could not get into the last ball or was out of countenance in the drawing room the last 80 Sunday of her appearance there. For none rail at the court but those who cannot get into it or else who are ridiculous when they are there, and I shall suspect you were laughed at when you were last there or would be a maid of honor.

OLIVIA.

I a maid of honor! To be a maid of honor were yet of all 85 things my aversion.

ELIZA.

In what sense am I to understand you? But in fine by the word aversion I'm sure you dissemble, for I never knew woman yet that used it who did not. Come, our tongues belie our hearts more than our pocket-glasses do our faces; 90 but methinks we ought to leave off dissembling, since 'tis grown of no use to us; for all wise observers understand us nowadays as they do dreams, almanacs, and Dutch gazettes, by the contrary. And a man no more believes a woman when she says she has an aversion for him than when she 95 says she'll cry out.

OLIVIA.

O filthy, hideous! Peace, cousin, or your discourse will be my aversion, and you may believe me.

ELIZA.

Yes, for if anything be a woman's aversion 'tis plain dealing from another woman, and perhaps that's your quarrel to 100 the world, for that will talk as your woman says.

OLIVIA.

Talk not of me sure, for what men do I converse with? What visits do I admit?

Enter Boy.

BOY.

Here's the gentleman to wait upon you, madam.

95. she says] *Q 1, Q 3–8, O; om. Q 2.*

OLIVIA.

On me! You little, unthinking fop, d'ye know what you 105
say?

BOY.

Yes, madam, 'tis the gentleman that comes every day to you,
who—

OLIVIA.

Hold your peace, you heedless little animal, and get you
gone. This country boy, cousin, takes my dancing-master, 110
tailor, or the spruce milliner for visitors.   *Exit* Boy.

LETTICE.

No, madam, 'tis Mr. Novel, I'm sure, by his talking so loud.
I know his voice too, madam.

OLIVIA.

You know nothing, you buffle-headed, stupid creature you.
You would make my cousin believe I receive visits. But if it 115
be Mr.—what did you call him?

LETTICE.

Mr. Novel, madam, he that—

OLIVIA.

Hold your peace, I'll hear no more of him. But if it be your
Mr. (I can't think of his name again) I suppose he has
followed my cousin hither.   120

ELIZA.

No, cousin, I will not rob you of the honor of the visit. 'Tis
to you, cousin, for I know him not.

OLIVIA.

Nor did I ever hear of him before, upon my honor, cousin.
Besides, ha'nt I told you that visits and the business of visits,
flattery, and detraction are my aversion? D'ye think then I 125
would admit such a coxcomb as he is, who rather than not
rail will rail at the dead whom none speak ill of, and rather
than not flatter will flatter the poets of the age, whom none
will flatter, who affects novelty as much as the fashion and
is as fantastical as changeable and as well known as the 130
fashion, who likes nothing but what is new, nay would
choose to have his friend or his title a new one. In fine, he is
my aversion.

ELIZA.

I find you do know him, cousin, at least have heard of him.

OLIVIA.

Yes, now I remember, I have heard of him.   135

ELIZA.

Well, but since he is such a coxcomb, for heaven's sake let him not come up. Tell him, Mrs. Lettice, your lady is not within.

OLIVIA.

No, Lettice, tell him my cousin is here and that he may come up, for, notwithstanding I detest the sight of him, you 140 may like his conversation, and though I would use him scurvily, I will not be rude to you in my own lodging. Since he has followed you hither, let him come up, I say.

ELIZA.

Very fine! Pray let him go to the devil, I say, for me. I know him not nor desire it. Send him away, Mrs. Lettice.   145

OLIVIA.

Upon my word, she shan't. I must disobey your commands, to comply with your desires. Call him up, Lettice.

ELIZA.

Nay, I'll swear she shall not stir on that errand.

Holds Lettice.

OLIVIA.

Well then, I'll call him myself for you, since you will have it so. (*Calls out at the door.*) Mr. Novel, sir, sir.   150

Enter Novel.

NOVEL.

Madam, I beg your pardon. Perhaps you were busy. I did not think you had company with you.

ELIZA (*aside*).

Yet he comes to me, cousin!

OLIVIA.

—Chairs there.   *They sit.*

NOVEL.

Well, but, madam, d'ye know whence I come now?   155

OLIVIA.

From some melancholy place I warrant, sir, since they have lost your good company.

150. S.D. *out*] *Q 1–7, O; om. Q 8.*

ELIZA.

> So.

NOVEL.

> From a place where they have treated me, at dinner, with
> so much civility and kindness, a pox on them, that I could 160
> hardly get away to you, dear madam.

OLIVIA.

> You have a way with you so new and obliging, sir.

ELIZA (*apart to* Olivia).

> You hate flattery, cousin!

NOVEL.

> Nay faith, madam, d'ye think my way new? Then you are
> obliging, madam. I must confess I hate imitation, to do 165
> anything like other people. All that know me do me the
> honor to say I am an original, faith. But, as I was saying,
> madam, I have been treated today with all the ceremony
> and kindness imaginable at my Lady Autum's, but the
> nauseous old woman at the upper end of her table—   170

OLIVIA.

> Revives the old Grecian custom of serving in a death's head
> with their banquets.

NOVEL.

> Hah, ha! Fine! Just, i'faith, nay, and new. 'Tis like eating
> with the ghost in the *Libertine*. She would frighten a man
> from her dinner with her hollow invitations, and spoil one's 175
> stomach—

OLIVIA.

> To meat or women. I detest her hollow cherry cheeks. She
> looks like an old coach new painted, affecting an unseemly
> smugness whilst she is ready to drop in pieces.

ELIZA (*apart to* Olivia).

> You hate detraction I see, cousin!   180

NOVEL.

> But the silly old fury, whilst she affects to look like a woman
> of this age, talks—

175. invitations] *Q1–5, Q8, O;*
invitation *Q6–7.*

---

174. *the Libertine*] Shadwell's play based on the Don Juan legend.

OLIVIA.

Like one of the last, and as passionately as an old courtier
who has outlived his office.

NOVEL.

Yes, madam, but pray let me give you her character. Then, 185
she never counts her age by the years but—

OLIVIA.

By the masques she has lived to see.

NOVEL.

Nay then, madam, I see you think a little harmless railing
too great a pleasure for any but yourself and therefore I've
done.   190

OLIVIA.

Nay, faith, you shall tell me who you had there at dinner.

NOVEL.

If you would hear me, madam.

OLIVIA.

Most patiently. Speak, sir.

NOVEL.

Then, we had her daughter—

OLIVIA.

Ay, her daughter, the very disgrace to good clothes, which 195
she always wears but to heighten her deformity, not mend
it. For she is still most splendidly, gallantly ugly and looks
like an ill piece of daubing in a rich frame.

NOVEL.

So! But have you done with her, madam? And can you
spare her to me a little now?   200

OLIVIA.

Ay, ay, sir.

NOVEL.

Then, she is like—

OLIVIA.

She is, you'd say, like a City bride, the greater fortune but
not the greater beauty for her dress.

NOVEL.

Well, yet have you done, madam? Then, she—   205

OLIVIA.

Then she bestows as unfortunately on her face all the graces
in fashion, as the languishing eye, the hanging or pouting

lip; but as the fool is never more provoking than when he
aims at wit, the ill-favored of our sex are never more
nauseous than when they would be beauties, adding to their 210
natural deformity, the artificial ugliness of affectation.

ELIZA.

So, cousin, I find one may have a collection of all one's
acquaintances' pictures as well at your house as at Mr.
Lely's. Only the difference is, there we find them much
handsomer than they are and like; here, much uglier and 215
like. And you are the first of the profession of picture-
drawing I ever knew without flattery.

OLIVIA.

I draw after the life, do nobody wrong, cousin.

ELIZA.

No, you hate flattery and detraction!

OLIVIA.

But, Mr. Novel, who had you besides at dinner?   220

NOVEL.

Nay, the devil take me if I tell you, unless you will allow me
the privilege of railing in my turn; but, now I think on't,
the women ought to be your province, as the men are mine.
And you must know, we had him whom—

OLIVIA.

Him, whom—   225

NOVEL.

What? Invading me already? And giving the character
before you know the man?

ELIZA.

No, that is not fair, though it be usual.

OLIVIA.

I beg your pardon, Mr. Novel, pray, go on.

NOVEL.

Then, I say, we had that familiar coxcomb, who is at home 230
wheresoe'er he comes.

OLIVIA.

Ay, that fool—

223. women] *Q1–2*, *Q4–8*, *O*;
woman *Q3*.

NOVEL.

Nay then, madam, your servant. I'm gone. Taking a fool out of one's mouth is worse than taking the bread out of one's mouth.   235

OLIVIA.

I've done. Your pardon, Mr. Novel, pray proceed.

NOVEL.

I say, the rogue, that he may be the only wit in the company, will let nobody else talk, and—

OLIVIA.

Ay, those fops who love to talk all themselves are of all things my aversion.   240

NOVEL.

Then you'll let me speak, madam, sure. The rogue, I say, will force his jest upon you, and I hate a jest that's forced upon a man as much as a glass.

ELIZA.

Why, I hope, sir, he does not expect a man of your temperance in jesting should do him reason?   245

NOVEL.

What, interruption from this side too! I must then—

Offers to rise, Olivia *holds him.*

OLIVIA.

No, sir— You must know, cousin, that fop he means, though he talks only to be commended, will not give you leave to do it.

NOVEL.

But, madam—   250

OLIVIA.

He a wit! Hang him, he's only an adopter of straggling jests and fatherless lampoons, by the credit of which he eats at good tables and so, like the barren beggar-woman, lives by borrowed children.

NOVEL.

Madam—   255

233. a fool] *Q1–7;* the fool *Q8, O.*   251. straggling] *Q1–2, Q4–8, O;*
246. then—] *Q1, Q6–7, O;* the—   strangling *Q3.*
Q2–5, Q8.

OLIVIA.

And never was author of anything but his news, but that is
still all his own.

NOVEL.

Madam, pray—

OLIVIA.

An eternal babbler, and makes no more use of his ears than
a man that sits at a play by his mistress or in fop-corner. 260
He's, in fine, a base, detracting fellow, and is my aversion.
But who else prithee, Mr. Novel, was there with you? Nay,
you shan't stir.

NOVEL.

I beg your pardon, madam, I cannot stay in any place
where I'm not allowed a little Christian liberty of railing. 265

OLIVIA.

Nay, prithee, Mr. Novel, stay, and, though you should rail
at me, I would hear you with patience. Prithee, who else
was there with you?

NOVEL.

Your servant, madam.

OLIVIA.

Nay, prithee tell us, Mr. Novel, prithee do.   270

NOVEL.

We had nobody else.

OLIVIA.

Nay, faith I know you had. Come, my Lord Plausible was
there too, who is, cousin, a—

ELIZA.

You need not tell me what he is, cousin, for I know him to
be a civil, good-natured, harmless gentleman, that speaks 275
well of all the world, and is always in good humor, and—

OLIVIA.

Hold, cousin, hold. I hate detraction, but I must tell you,
cousin, his civility is cowardice, his good nature want of wit;
and has neither courage or sense to rail. And for his being

279. and] *Q 1–5, Q 8, O*; and he   279. or] *Q 1–3, O*; nor *Q 4–8.
Q 6–7.*

260. *fop-corner*] section of the pit popular with the young-men-about-
town.

always in humor, 'tis because he is never dissatisfied with 280
himself. In fine, he is my aversion, and I never admit his
visits beyond my hall.

NOVEL.

No, he visit you! Damn him, cringing, grinning rogue. If I
should see him coming up to you, I would make bold to
kick him down again. Ha!—   285

Enter my Lord Plausible.

My dear lord, your most humble servant.

Rises and salutes Plausible *and kisses him.*

ELIZA (*aside*).

So! I find kissing and railing succeed each other with the
angry men as well as with the angry women, and their
quarrels are like love quarrels, since absence is the only
cause of them; for as soon as the man appears again, they 290
are over.

LORD PLAUSIBLE.

Your most faithful, humble servant, generous Mr. Novel,
and, madam, I am your eternal slave and kiss your fair
hands, which I had done sooner, according to your commands, but—   295

OLIVIA.

No excuses, my lord.

ELIZA (*apart*).

What, you sent for him then, cousin?

NOVEL (*aside*).

Ha! Invited!

OLIVIA.

I know you must divide yourself, for your good company is
too general a good to be engrossed by any particular friend. 300

LORD PLAUSIBLE.

O Lord, madam, my company! Your most obliged, faithful,
humble servant, but I could have brought you good company indeed, for I parted at your door with two of the
worthiest, bravest men—

OLIVIA.

Who were they, my lord?   305

284. see] *Q1–7, O;* meet *Q8.*

NOVEL.

Who do you call the worthiest, bravest men, pray?

LORD PLAUSIBLE.

O the wisest, bravest gentlemen! Men of such honor and
virtue! Of such good qualities! Ah—

ELIZA (*aside*).

This is a coxcomb that speaks ill of all people a different
way and libels everybody with dull praise, and commonly 310
in the wrong place, so makes his panegyrics abusive lampoons.

OLIVIA.

But pray let me know who they were.

LORD PLAUSIBLE.

Ah! Such patterns of heroic virtue! Such—

NOVEL.

Well, but who the devil were they?   315

LORD PLAUSIBLE.

The honor of our nation, the glory of our age. Ah! I could
dwell a twelvemonth on their praise, which indeed I might
spare by telling their names: Sir John Current and Sir
Richard Court-Title.

NOVEL.

Court-Title! Hah, ha.   320

OLIVIA.

And Sir John Current! Why will you keep such a wretch
company, my lord?

LORD PLAUSIBLE.

Oh, madam, seriously you are a little too severe, for he is a
man of unquestioned reputation in everything.

OLIVIA.

Yes, because he endeavors only with the women to pass for 325
a man of courage and with the bullies for a wit, with the
wits for a man of business, and with the men of business for
a favorite at court, and at court for good city security.

NOVEL.

And for Sir Richard, he—

LORD PLAUSIBLE.

He loves your choice, picked company, persons that—   330

OLIVIA.

He loves a lord indeed, but—

NOVEL.

Pray, dear madam, let me have but a bold stroke or two at
his picture. He loves a lord as you say though—

OLIVIA.

Though he borrowed his money and ne'er paid him again.

NOVEL.

And would bespeak a place three days before at the back 335
end of a lord's coach to Hyde Park.

LORD PLAUSIBLE.

Nay, i'faith, i'faith, you are both too severe.

OLIVIA.

Then, to show yet more his passion for quality, he makes
love to that fulsome coach-load of honor, my Lady Goodly,
for he is always at her lodging.   340

LORD PLAUSIBLE.

Because it is the conventicle-gallant, the meetinghouse of
all the fair ladies and glorious, superfine beauties of the
town.

NOVEL.

Very fine ladies! There's first—

OLIVIA.

Her honor, as fat as an hostess.   345

LORD PLAUSIBLE.

She is something plump indeed, a goodly, comely, graceful
person.

NOVEL.

Then there's my Lady Frances, what d'ye call her? As
ugly—

OLIVIA.

As a citizen's lawfully begotten daughter.   350

LORD PLAUSIBLE.

She has wit in abundance, and the handsomest heel, elbow,
and tip of an ear you ever saw.

NOVEL.

Heel and elbow! Hah, ha! And there's my Lady Betty you
know—

OLIVIA.

As sluttish and slatternly as an Irishwoman bred in France. 355

LORD PLAUSIBLE.

Ah, all she has hangs with a loose air indeed and becoming
negligence.

ELIZA.

You see all faults with lover's eyes, I find, my lord.

LORD PLAUSIBLE.

Ah, madam, your most obliged, faithful, humble servant to
command! But you can say nothing sure against the super- 360
fine mistress—

OLIVIA.

I know who you mean. She is as censorious and detracting
a jade as a superannuated sinner.

LORD PLAUSIBLE.

She has a smart way of raillery, 'tis confessed.

NOVEL.

And then, for Mrs. Grideline.   365

LORD PLAUSIBLE.

She I'm sure is—

OLIVIA.

One that never spoke ill of anybody, 'tis confessed, for she
is as silent in conversation as a country lover and no
better company than a clock or a weather-glass, for if she
sounds 'tis but once an hour to put you in mind of the time 370
of day or to tell you 'twill be cold or hot, rain or snow.

LORD PLAUSIBLE.

Ah, poor creature! She's extremely good and modest.

NOVEL.

And for Mrs. Bridlechin, she's—

OLIVIA.

As proud as a churchman's wife.

LORD PLAUSIBLE.

She's a woman of great spirit and honor and will not make 375
herself cheap, 'tis true.

NOVEL.

Then Mrs. Hoyden, that calls all people by their surnames
and is—

OLIVIA.

As familiar a duck—

NOVEL.

As an actress in the tiring room. There, I was once before- 380
hand with you, madam.

---

371. or to tell] *Q 1, O*; or tell *Q 2–8*.

LORD PLAUSIBLE.

Mrs. Hoyden! A poor, affable, good-natured soul! But the divine Mrs. Trifle comes thither too. Sure her beauty, virtue, and conduct you can say nothing to.

OLIVIA.

No! 385

NOVEL.

No!—Pray let me speak, madam.

OLIVIA.

First, can anyone be called beautiful that squints?

LORD PLAUSIBLE.

Her eyes languish a little, I own.

NOVEL.

Languish! Hah, ha.

OLIVIA.

Languish! Then for her conduct she was seen at *The* 390 *Country Wife* after the first day. There's for you, my lord.

LORD PLAUSIBLE.

But, madam, she was not seen to use her fan all the play long, turn aside her head, or by a conscious blush discover more guilt than modesty.

OLIVIA.

Very fine! Then you think a woman modest that sees the 395 hideous *Country Wife* without blushing or publishing her detestation of it? D'ye hear him, cousin?

ELIZA.

Yes, and am, I must confess, something of his opinion and think that as an over-conscious fool at a play, by en- deavoring to show the author's want of wit, exposes his 400 own to more censure, so may a lady call her modesty in question by publicly caviling with the poets; for all those grimaces of honor and artificial modesty disparage a woman's real virtue as much as the use of white and red does the natural complexion, and you must use very, very 405 little if you would have it thought your own.

OLIVIA.

Then you would have a woman of honor with passive looks,

384. to] *Q4–8, O*; too *Q1–3.*

390–391. *The Country Wife*] Wycherley's third play, decidedly for adult audiences.

ears, and tongue undergo all the hideous obscenity she
hears at nasty plays?

ELIZA.

Truly I think a woman betrays her want of modesty by show- 410
ing it publicly in a playhouse as much as a man does his
want of courage by a quarrel there, for the truly modest and
stout say least and are least exceptious, especially in public.

OLIVIA.

O hideous! Cousin, this cannot be your opinion, but you
are one of those who have the confidence to pardon the 415
filthy play.

ELIZA.

Why, what is there of ill in it, say you?

OLIVIA.

O fie, fie, fie, would you put me to the blush anew? Call all
the blood into my face again? But to satisfy you then, first,
the clandestine obscenity in the very name of Horner.   420

ELIZA.

Truly, 'tis so hidden I cannot find it out, I confess.

OLIVIA.

O horrid! Does it not give you the rank conception or
image of a goat, a town-bull, or a satyr? Nay, what is yet a
filthier image than all the rest, that of an eunuch?

ELIZA.

What then? I can think of a goat, a bull, or satyr without 425
any hurt.

OLIVIA.

Ay, but, cousin, one cannot stop there.

ELIZA.

I can, cousin.

OLIVIA.

O no, for when you have those filthy creatures in your head
once, the next thing you think is what they do, as their 430
defiling of honest men's beds and couches, rapes upon

422. it not] *Q1, Q4–8, O*; not it   bull *Q3–8, O.*
Q2–3.   425. or] *Q1–7*; or a *Q8, O.*
423. a town-bull] *Q1–2*; or town-

420. *Horner*] leading character in *The Country Wife*, whose name does
indeed suggest a principal occupation.

sleeping and waking country virgins under hedges and on haycocks. Nay, farther—

ELIZA.

Nay, no farther, cousin. We have enough of your comment on the play, which will make me more ashamed than the 435 play itself.

OLIVIA.

O, believe me, 'tis a filthy play, and you may take my word for a filthy play, as soon as another's, but the filthiest thing in that play, or any other play, is—

ELIZA.

Pray keep it to yourself, if it be so.   440

OLIVIA.

No, faith, you shall know it. I'm resolved to make you out of love with the play. I say, the lewdest, filthiest thing is his china. Nay, I will never forgive the beastly author his china. He has quite taken away the reputation of poor china itself and sullied the most innocent and pretty furniture of a 445 lady's chamber, insomuch that I was fain to break all my defiled vessels. You see I have none left; nor you, I hope.

ELIZA.

You'll pardon me, I cannot think the worse of my china for that of the playhouse.

OLIVIA.

Why, you will not keep any now sure! 'Tis now as unfit an 450 ornament for a lady's chamber as the pictures that come from Italy and other hot countries, as appears by their nudities, which I always cover or scratch out, wheresoe'er I find them. But china! Out upon it, filthy china, nasty, debauched china!   455

ELIZA.

All this will not put me out of conceit with china nor the play, which is acted today or another of the same beastly author's, as you call him, which I'll go see.

OLIVIA.

You will not sure! Nay, you shall not venture your reputa-

434. farther—] Q1; further— Q2–   443. forgive] Q1–3; forget Q4–8, O.
8, O.   453. scratch] Q1–2, Q6; O; search
435. me] Q1–5, Q8, O; you Q6–7.   Q3–5, Q8; snatch Q7.

tion by going and mine by leaving me alone with two men   460
here. Nay, you'll disoblige me forever, if—   *Pulls her back.*

ELIZA.

I stay!—your servant.   *Exit* Eliza.

OLIVIA.

Well—but my lord, though you justify everybody, you
cannot in earnest uphold so beastly a writer, whose ink is
so smutty, as one may say.   465

LORD PLAUSIBLE.

Faith, I dare swear the poor man did not think to disoblige
the ladies by any amorous, soft, passionate, luscious saying
in his play.

OLIVIA.

Foy, my lord, but what think you, Mr. Novel, of the play?
Though I know you are a friend to all that are new.   470

NOVEL.

Faith, madam, I must confess the new plays would not be
the worse for my advice but I could never get the silly rogues,
the poets, to mind what I say; but I'll tell you what counsel
I gave the surly fool you speak of.

OLIVIA.

What was it?   475

NOVEL.

Faith, to put his play into rime, for rime, you know, often
makes mystical nonsense pass with the critics for wit, and a
double-meaning saying with the ladies for soft, tender, and
moving passion. But, now I talk of passion, I saw your old
lover this morning—Captain—   *Whispers.* 480

Enter Captain Manly, Freeman *and* Fidelia *standing behind.*

OLIVIA.

Whom?—Nay, you need not whisper.

MANLY.

We are luckily got hither unobserved. —How! In a close

469. Foy] *Q 1–4, O;* Fy *Q 5–7;* Fie   474. speak] *Q 1–2;* spake *Q 3–6,*
Q 8.   *Q 8, O;* spoke *Q 7.*
470. a friend] *Q 1–2, Q 4–8, O;* my   476. rime] *Q 1–3;* rithme *Q 4–7;*
friend *Q 3.*   rhyme *Q 8, O.*

469. *Foy*] from the French expression *ma foi.*

conversation with these supple rascals, the outcasts of
sempstresses' shops?

FREEMAN.

Faith, pardon her, captain, that, since she could no longer 485
be entertained with your manly bluntness and honest love,
she takes up with the pert chat and commonplace flattery
of these fluttering parrots of the town, apes and echoes of
men only.

MANLY.

Do not you, sir, play the echo too, mock me, dally with my 490
own words and show yourself as impertinent as they are.

FREEMAN.

Nay, captain—

FIDELIA.

Nay, lieutenant, do not excuse her. Methinks she looks very
kindly upon them both and seems to be pleased with what
that fool there says to her.   495

MANLY.

You lie, sir, and hold your peace that I may not be provoked
to give you a worse reply.

OLIVIA.

Manly returned, d'ye say? And is he safe?

NOVEL.

My lord saw him too.   (*Whispers to* Plausible.)   Hark you,
my lord.   500

MANLY (*aside*).

She yet seems concerned for my safety and perhaps they are
admitted now here but for their news of me, for intelligence
indeed is the common passport of nauseous fools when they
go their round of good tables and houses.

OLIVIA.

I heard of his fighting only, without particulars, and confess 505
I always loved his brutal courage because it made me hope
it might rid me of his more brutal love.

MANLY (*apart*).

What's that?

490. dally] *Q1, Q4–8, O;* dully   *Q8, O; entire speech om. Q6–7.*
Q2–3.   501. *aside] Q1–6, Q8, O; om. Q7.*
499–500. My lord ... lord] *Q1–5,*

OLIVIA.

But is he at last returned, d'ye say, unhurt?

NOVEL.

Ay faith, without doing his business, for the rogue has been 510
these two years pretending to a wooden leg, which he
would take from fortune as kindly as the staff of a marshal
of France and rather read his name in a gazette—

OLIVIA.

Than in the entail of a good estate.

MANLY (*aside*).

So!— 515

NOVEL.

I have an ambition, I must confess, of losing my heart before
such a fair enemy as yourself, madam, but that silly rogues
should be ambitious of losing their arms and—

OLIVIA.

Looking like a pair of compasses.

NOVEL.

But he has no use of his arms but to set them on kimbow, 520
for he never pulls off his hat, at least not to me, I'm sure,
for you must know, madam, he has a fanatical hatred to
good company. He can't abide me.

LORD PLAUSIBLE.

O, be not so severe to him as to say he hates good company,
for I assure you he has a great respect, esteem, and kindness 525
for me.

MANLY.

That kind, civil rogue has spoken yet ten thousand times
worse of me than t'other.

OLIVIA.

Well, if he be returned, Mr. Novel, then shall I be pestered
again with his boisterous sea love, have my alcove smell like 530
a cabin, my chamber perfumed with his tarpaulin Brandenburgh, and hear volleys of brandy sighs enough to make a

514. Than] *Q 1–2, Q 4–8, O*; Then   522. fanatical] *Q 1–2, Q 8, O*; fan-
Q 3.   tastical *Q 3–7.*

520. *on kimbow*] akimbo.
531–532. *Brandenburgh*] dressing gown.

fog in one's room. Foh! I hate a lover that smells like
Thames Street!

MANLY (*aside*).

I can bear no longer and need hear no more. [*Aloud.*] 535
But, since you have these two pulvillio boxes, these essence
bottles, this pair of muskcats here, I hope I may venture to
come yet nearer you.

OLIVIA.

Overheard us then?

NOVEL (*aside*).

I hope he heard me not.   540

LORD PLAUSIBLE.

Most noble and heroic captain, your most obliged, faithful,
humble servant.

NOVEL.

Dear tar, thy humble servant.

MANLY.

Away—madam!

> *Thrusts* Novel *and* Plausible *on each side.*

OLIVIA.

Nay, I think I have fitted you for listening.   545

MANLY.

You have fitted me for believing you could not be fickle
though you were young, could not dissemble love though
'twas your interest, nor be vain though you were handsome,
nor break your promise though to a parting lover, nor abuse
your best friend though you had wit. But I take not your 550
contempt of me worse than your esteem or civility for these
things here though you know them.

NOVEL.

Things!

LORD PLAUSIBLE.

Let the captain railly a little.

MANLY.

Yes, things. Can'st thou be angry, thou thing?   555

> *Coming up to* Novel.

544.1. *Thrusts . . . side*] *after l. 591*   548. be] *Q 3–8, O*; be in *Q 1–2.*
in Q 1–8, O.   551. for] *Q 1–5, Q 8, O*; of *Q 6–7.*
547. not] *Q 1–6, Q 8, O; om. Q 7.*

536. *pulvillio*] scented powder.

NOVEL.

No, since my lord says you speak in raillery, for, though your
sea raillery be something rough, yet I confess we use one
another too as bad every day at Locket's and never quarrel
for the matter.

LORD PLAUSIBLE.

Nay, noble captain, be not angry with him. A word with 560
you, I beseech you—   *Whispers to* Manly.

OLIVIA (*aside*).

Well, we women, like the rest of the cheats of the world,
when our cullies or creditors have found us out and will
or can trust no longer, pay debts, and satisfy obligations
with a quarrel, the kindest present a man can make to his 565
mistress when he can make no more presents. For often-
times in love as at cards we are forced to play foul, only to
give over the game, and use our lovers, like the cards, when
we can get no more by them, throw them up in a pet upon
the first dispute.   570

MANLY.

My lord, all that you have made me know by your whisper-
ing, which I knew not before, is that you have a stinking
breath. There's a secret for your secret.

LORD PLAUSIBLE.

Pshaw! Pshaw!

MANLY.

But, madam, tell me, pray, what was it about this spark 575
could take you? Was it the merit of his fashionable impudence, the briskness of his noise, the wit of his laugh, his
judgment or fancy in his garniture? Or was it a well-
trimmed glove or the scent of it that charmed you?

NOVEL.

Very well, sir. Gad, these sea captains make nothing of 580
dressing. But let me tell you, sir, a man by his dress as much
as by anything shows his wit and judgment, nay, and his
courage too.

FREEMAN.

How his courage, Mr. Novel?

---

559. for] *Q 1–7, O*; at *Q 8*.   567. are] *Q 1–4, Q 8, O*; were *Q 5–7*.

---

558. *Locket's*] restaurant at Charing Cross.

NOVEL.

Why, for example, by red breeches, tucked-up hair or 585
peruke, a greasy broad belt, and nowadays a short sword.

MANLY.

Thy courage will appear more by thy belt than thy sword, I
dare swear. Then, madam, for this gentle piece of courtesy,
this man of tame honor, what could you find in him? Was
it his languishing affected tone? His mannerly look? His 590
secondhand flattery, the refuse of the playhouse tiring
rooms? Or his slavish obsequiousness in watching at the
door of your box at the playhouse for your hand to your
chair? Or his jaunty way of playing with your fan? Or was
it the gunpowder spot on his hand or the jewel in his ear 595
that purchased your heart?

OLIVIA.

Good jealous captain, no more of your—

LORD PLAUSIBLE.

No, let him go on, madam, for perhaps he may make you
laugh, and I would contribute to your pleasure any way.

MANLY.

Gentle rogue!
600

OLIVIA.

No, noble captain, you cannot sure think anything could
take me more than that heroic title of yours, captain, for
you know we women love honor inordinately.

NOVEL.

Hah, ha, faith she is with thee, bully, for thy raillery.

MANLY (*aside to* Novel).

Faith so shall I be with you, no bully, for your grinning. 605

OLIVIA.

Then, that noble lionlike mien of yours, that soldierlike,
weather-beaten complexion, and that manly roughness of
your voice, how can they otherwise than charm us women,
who hate effeminacy!

NOVEL.

Hah, ha! Faith I can't hold from laughing.
610

MANLY (*aside to* Novel).

Nor shall I from kicking anon.

OLIVIA.

And then, that captain-like carelessness in your dress, but

especially your scarf. 'Twas just such another, only a little
higher tied, made me in love with my tailor as he passed by
my window the last training day, for we women adore a 615
martial man, and you have nothing wanting to make you
more one, or more agreeable, but a wooden leg.

LORD PLAUSIBLE.

Nay, i'faith there your ladyship was a wag, and it was fine,
just, and well raillied.

NOVEL.

Ay, ay, madam, with you ladies too martial men must 620
needs be very killing.

MANLY.

Peace, you Bartholomew-Fair buffoons, and be not you vain
that these laugh on your side, for they will laugh at their own
dull jests. But no more of them, for I will only suffer now
this lady to be witty and merry.   625

OLIVIA.

You would not have your panegyric interrupted. I go on
then to your humor. Is there anything more agreeable than
the pretty sullenness of that? Than the greatness of your
courage, which most of all appears in your spirit of contra-
diction, for you dare give all mankind the lie, and your 630
opinion is your only mistress, for you renounce that too when
it becomes another man's.

NOVEL.

Hah, ha! I cannot hold. I must laugh at thee, tar, faith!

LORD PLAUSIBLE.

And i'faith, dear captain, I beg your pardon and leave to
laugh at you too, though I protest I mean you no hurt, but 635
when a lady raillies, a stander-by must be complaisant and
do her reason in laughing. Hah, ha.

MANLY.

Why, you impudent, pitiful wretches, you presume sure
upon your effeminacy to urge me, for you are in all things
so like women that you may think it in me a kind of 640
cowardice to beat you.

---

622. *Bartholomew-Fair*] the popular fair held in Smithfield every August,
famed for drolls, puppet shows, and the like.

OLIVIA.

No hectoring, good captain.

MANLY.

Or perhaps you think this lady's presence secures you, but
have a care, she has talked herself out of all the respect I had
for her, and by using me ill before you has given me a 645
privilege of using you so before her, but if you would preserve your respect to her and not be beaten before her, go,
be gone immediately.

NOVEL.

Be gone! What!

LORD PLAUSIBLE.

Nay, worthy, noble, generous captain.   650

MANLY.

Be gone, I say.

NOVEL.

Be gone again! To us be gone!

MANLY.

No chattering, baboons, instantly be gone. Or—

       Manly *puts them out of the room*: Novel *struts*, Plausible *cringes*.

NOVEL.

Well, madam, we'll go make the cards ready in your bedchamber. Sure you will not stay long with him.   655

           Exeunt Plausible, Novel.

OLIVIA.

Turn hither your rage, good Captain Swagger-huff, and be
saucy with your mistress, like a true captain. But be civil to
your rivals and betters and do not threaten anything but me
here, no, not so much as my windows, nor do not think
yourself in the lodgings of one of your suburb mistresses 660
beyond the Tower.

MANLY.

Do not give me cause to think so, for those less infamous
women part with their lovers, just as you did from me,
with unforced vows of constancy and floods of willing tears,
but the same winds bear away their lovers and their vows. 665
And for their grief, if the credulous, unexpected fools return,
they find new comforters, fresh cullies, such as I found here.
The mercenary love of those women too suffers shipwreck

668. suffers] *Q2–8, O*; suffer *Q1.*

with their gallants' fortunes. Now you have heard chance
has used me scurvily, therefore you do too. Well, persevere 670
in your ingratitude, falsehood, and disdain. Have constancy in something and I promise you to be as just to your
real scorn as I was to your feigned love, and henceforward
will despise, contemn, hate, loathe, and detest you, most
faithfully.   675

Enter Lettice.

OLIVIA.

Get the hombre cards ready in the next room, Lettice,
and—   *Whispers to* Lettice.

FREEMAN.

Bravely resolved, captain.

FIDELIA.

And you'll be sure to keep your word, I hope, sir.

MANLY.

I hope so too.   680

FIDELIA.

Do you but hope it, sir? If you are not as good as your word,
'twill be the first time you ever bragged sure.

MANLY.

She has restored my reason with my heart.

FREEMAN.

But, now you talk of restoring, captain, there are other
things which, next to one's heart, one would not part with. 685
I mean your jewels and money, which it seems she has, sir.

MANLY.

What's that to you, sir?

FREEMAN.

Pardon me, whatsoever is yours, I have a share in it, I'm
sure, which I will not lose for asking, though you may be
too generous, or too angry now to do it yourself.   690

FIDELIA.

Nay, then I'll make bold to make my claim too.
                                Both going towards Olivia.

MANLY.

Hold, you impertinent, officious fops— (*Aside.*) How have
I been deceived?

691. my] *Q 1–5, Q 8, O; om. Q 6–7.*

FREEMAN.

Madam, there are certain appurtenances to a lover's heart,
called jewels, which always go along with it.   695

FIDELIA.

And which, with lovers, have no value in themselves but
from the heart they come with. Our captain's, madam, it
seems you scorn to keep, and much more will those worthless
things without it, I am confident.

OLIVIA.

A gentleman so well made as you are may be confident—us 700
easy women could not deny you anything you ask, if'twere
for yourself; but, since 'tis for another, I beg your leave to
give him my answer. (*Aside.*) An agreeable young fellow
this!—And would not be my aversion! (*To* Manly.)
Captain, your young friend here has a very persuading face, 705
I confess; yet you might have asked me yourself for those
trifles you left with me, which (hark you a little, for I dare
trust you with the secret; you are a man of so much honor,
I'm sure), I say then, not expecting your return or hoping
ever to see you again, I have delivered your jewels to—   710

MANLY.

Whom?

OLIVIA.

My husband.

MANLY.

Your husband!

OLIVIA.

Ay, my husband, for, since you could leave me, I am lately
and privately married to one who is a man of so much 715
honor and experience in the world that I dare not ask him
for your jewels again to restore them to you, lest he should
conclude you never would have parted with them to me, on
any other score but the exchange of my honor, which rather
than you'd let me lose, you'd lose I'm sure yourself those 720
trifles of yours.

MANLY.

Triumphant impudence! But married too!

717. should] *Q 1–2, O;* could *Q 3–8.*   719. but] *Q 1–7, O;* but upon *Q 8.*

OLIVIA.

O, speak not so loud. My servants know it not. I am married. There's no resisting one's destiny, or love, you know.

MANLY.

Why, did you love him too?   725

OLIVIA.

Most passionately, nay, love him now, though I have married him, and he me. Which mutual love, I hope you are too good, too generous a man to disturb by any future claim or visits to me. 'Tis true he is now absent in the country but returns shortly. Therefore, I beg of you, for your own ease 730 and quiet and my honor, you will never see me more.

MANLY.

I wish I never had seen you.

OLIVIA.

But if you should ever have any thing to say to me hereafter, let that young gentleman there be your messenger.

MANLY.

You would be kinder to him. I find he should be welcome. 735

OLIVIA.

Alas, his youth would keep my husband from suspicions and his visits from scandal, for we women may have pity for such as he but no love. And I already think you do not well to spirit him away to sea, and the sea is already but too rich with the spoils of the shore.   740

MANLY (aside).

True perfect woman! If I could say anything more injurious to her now, I would, for I could out-rail a bilked whore or a kicked coward, but, now I think on it, that were rather to discover my love than hatred, and I must not talk, for something I must do.   745

OLIVIA (aside).

I think I have given him enough of me now never to be troubled with him again.

Enter Lettice.

Well, Lettice, are the cards and all ready within? I come

732. never had] Q1–7; had never   739. is already] Q1–7, O; already
Q8, O.   is Q8.

---

then. Captain, I beg your pardon. You will not make one
at hombre? 750
MANLY.

No, madam, but I'll wish you a little good luck before you
go.
OLIVIA.

No, if you would have me thrive, curse me, for that you'll
do heartily, I suppose.
MANLY.

Then, if you will have it so, may all the curses light upon 755
you, women ought to fear and you deserve. First may the
curse of loving play attend your sordid covetousness and
fortune cheat you by trusting to her as you have cheated me;
the curse of pride or a good reputation fall on your lust; the
curse of affectation on your beauty; the curse of your hus- 760
band's company on your pleasures, and the curse of your
gallant's disappointments in his absence; and the curse of
scorn, jealousy, or despair on your love, and then the curse
of loving on.
OLIVIA.

And, to requite all your curses, I will only return you your 765
last. May the curse of loving me still fall upon your proud,
hard heart that could be so cruel to me in these horrid
curses, but heaven forgive you. *Exit* Olivia.
MANLY.

Hell and the devil reward thee.
FREEMAN.

Well, you see now mistresses, like friends, are lost by letting 770
them handle your money, and most women are such kind of
witches, who can have no power over a man unless you give
them money; but when once they have got any from you,
they never leave you, till they have all. Therefore I never
dare give a woman a farthing. 775
MANLY.

Well, there is yet this comfort: by losing one's money with
one's mistress a man is out of danger of getting another, of
being made prize again by love, who, like a pirate, takes you
by spreading false colors, but when once you have run your
ship aground, the treacherous picaroon loofs, so by your 780
ruin you save yourself from slavery at least.

Enter Boy.

BOY.

Mrs. Lettice, here's Madam Blackacre come to wait upon her honor.

MANLY.

D'ye hear that? Let us be gone before she comes, for hence-forward I'll avoid the whole damned sex forever and 785 woman as a sinking ship.   *Exeunt* Manly *and* Fidelia.

FREEMAN.

And I'll stay to revenge on her your quarrel to the sex, for out of love to her jointure and hatred to business I would marry her, to make an end of her thousand suits and my thousand engagements, to the comfort of two unfortunate 790 sorts of people: my plaintiffs and her defendants, my creditors and her adversaries.

Enter Widow Blackacre *led in by* Major Oldfox, *and* Jerry Blackacre *following, laden with green bags.*

WIDOW.

'Tis an arrant sea ruffian, but I am glad I met with him at last to serve him again, major, for the last service was not good in law. Boy, duck, Jerry, where is my paper of 795 memorandums? Give me, child. So. Where is my cousin Olivia now, my kind relation?

FREEMAN.

Here is one that would be your kind relation, madam.

WIDOW.

What mean you, sir?

FREEMAN.

Why, faith (to be short) to marry you, widow.   800

WIDOW.

Is not this the wild, rude person we saw at Captain Manly's?

JERRY.

Ay, forsooth, an't please.

WIDOW.

What would you? What are you? Marry me!

FREEMAN.

Ay, faith, for I am a younger brother and you are a widow.

WIDOW.

You are an impertinent person, and go about your business. 805

FREEMAN.

I have none but to marry thee, widow.

WIDOW.

But I have other business, I'd have you to know.

FREEMAN.

But you have no business anights, widow, and I'll make you pleasanter business than any you have. For anights, I assure you, I am a man of great business, for the business—   810

WIDOW.

Go, I'm sure you're an idle fellow.

FREEMAN.

Try me but, widow, and employ me as you find my abilities and industry.

OLDFOX.

Pray be civil to the lady, Mr. ——. She's a person of quality, a person that is no person—   815

FREEMAN.

Yes, but she's a person that is a widow. Be you mannerly to her because you are to pretend only to be her squire, to arm her to her lawyer's chambers; but I will be impudent and bawdy, for she must love and marry me.

WIDOW.

Marry come up, you saucy familiar Jack! You think with us 820
widows, 'tis no more than up and ride. Gad forgive me, nowadays every idle, young, hectoring, roaring companion with a pair of turned red breeches and a broad back thinks to carry away any widow of the best degree, but I'd have you to know, sir, all widows are not got, like places at court, 825
by impudence and importunity only.

OLDFOX.

No, no, soft, soft. You are a young man and not fit—

FREEMAN.

For a widow? Yes sure, old man, the fitter.

OLDFOX.

Go to, go to, if others had not laid in their claims before you—   830

FREEMAN.

Not you, I hope.

OLDFOX.

Why not I, sir? Sure I am a much more proportionable

match for her than you sir. I, who am an elder brother, of a
comfortable fortune and of equal years with her.

WIDOW.

How's that? You unmannerly person, I'd have you to know, 835
I was born but in *ann' undec' Caroli prim'*.

OLDFOX.

Your pardon, lady, your pardon. Be not offended with your
very servant. —But I say, sir, you are a beggarly younger
brother, twenty years younger than her, without any land or
stock but your great stock of impudence. Therefore what 840
pretension can you have to her?

FREEMAN.

You have made it for me. First, because I am a younger
brother.

WIDOW.

Why, is that a sufficient plea to a relict? How appears it,
sir? By what foolish custom? 845

FREEMAN.

By custom time out of mind only. Then, sir, because I have
nothing to keep me after her death, I am the likelier to take
care of her life. And, for my being twenty years younger
than her and having a sufficient stock of impudence, I
leave it to her whether they will be valid exceptions to me in 850
her widow's law or equity.

OLDFOX.

Well, she has been so long in chancery that I'll stand to her
equity and decree between us. Come, lady, pray snap up
this young snap at first or we shall be troubled with him.
Give him a city widow's answer—(*aside to the* Widow) that 855
is, with all the ill breeding imaginable. —Come, madam.

WIDOW.

Well then, to make an end of this foolish wooing, for nothing
interrupts business more. First, for you, major—

OLDFOX.

You declare in my favor then?

836. *undec.*] Q1-7, O; *decim* Q8.

---

836. *ann' undec' Caroli prim'*] If the widow gives the date, 1636, honestly
—she does give it characteristically, in the form of a statute—she would
be approximately thirty-eight years old (if the action is during the second
Dutch war), old enough to have a son of twenty-one.

FREEMAN.

What, direct the court? (*To* Jerry.) Come, young law- 860
yer, thou shalt be a counsel for me.

JERRY.

Gad, I shall betray your cause then as well as an older lawyer, never stir.

WIDOW.

First, I say, for you, major, my walking hospital of an
ancient foundation, thou bag of mummy that wouldst fall 865
asunder if 'twere not for thy cerecloths—

OLDFOX.

How, lady?

FREEMAN.

Hah, ha—

JERRY.

Hey, brave mother! Use all suitors thus, for my sake.

WIDOW.

Thou withered, hobbling, distorted cripple; nay, thou art 870
a cripple all over. Wouldst thou make me the staff of thy
age, the crutch of thy decrepitness? Me—

FREEMAN.

Well said, widow! Faith, thou wouldst make a man love
thee now without dissembling.

WIDOW.

Thou senseless, impertinent, quibbling, driveling, feeble, 875
paralytic, impotent, fumbling, frigid nincompoop.

JERRY.

Hey, brave mother for calling of names, ifac!

WIDOW.

Wouldst thou make a caudlemaker, a nurse of me? Can't
you be bedrid without a bedfellow? Won't your swanskins,
furs, flannels, and the scorched trencher keep you warm 880
there? Would you have me your Scotch warming pan, with
a pox to you? Me!—

876. frigid] *Q 1–7, O*; rigid *Q 8.*   candlemaker *Q 2.*
878. caudlemaker] *Q 1, Q 3–8, O*;

---

880. *scorched trencher*] heated platter, which like all the other devices,
including the wench referred to as a Scotch warming pan, would serve to
keep one warm in bed.

OLDFOX.

O heavens!

FREEMAN.

I told you I should be thought the fitter man, major.

JERRY.

Ay, you old fobus, and you would have been my guardian, 885
would you? To have taken care of my estate, that half of it
should never come to me, by letting long leases at peppercorn rents.

WIDOW.

If I would have married an old man, 'tis well known I
might have married an earl; nay, what's more, a judge and 890
been covered the winter nights with the lambskins which I
prefer to the ermines of nobles. And dost thou think I
would wrong my poor minor there for you?

FREEMAN.

Your minor is a chopping minor, God bless him.

Strokes Jerry *on the head.*

OLDFOX.

Your minor may be a major of horse or foot for his bigness, 895
and it seems you will have the cheating of your minor to
yourself.

WIDOW.

Pray, sir, bear witness. Cheat my minor! I'll bring my
action of the case for the slander.

FREEMAN.

Nay, I would bear false witness for thee now, widow, since 900
you have done me justice and have thought me the fitter
man for you.

WIDOW.

Fair and softly, sir. 'Tis my minor's case more than my own.
And I must do him justice now on you.

FREEMAN.

How?   905

---

885. *fobus*] Summers (*The Complete Works of William Wycherley* [London,
1924], II, 302) gives "old fool," from "to fob"—i.e., trick.
887–888. *peppercorn rents*] common token payment.
891. *lambskins*] used in judicial attire.

OLDFOX.

So then.

WIDOW.

You are first, I warrant, some renegado from the Inns of Court and the law, and thou'lt come to suffer for it by the law, that is, be hanged.

JERRY.

Not about your neck, forsooth, I hope. 910

FREEMAN.

But, madam—

OLDFOX.

Hear the court.

WIDOW.

Thou art some debauched, drunken, lewd, hectoring, gaming companion, and want'st some widow's old gold to nick upon, but I thank you, sir. That's for my lawyers. 915

FREEMAN.

Faith, we should ne'er quarrel about that, for guineas would serve my turn. But, widow—

WIDOW.

Thou art a foulmouthed boaster of thy lust, a mere braggadocio of thy strength for wine and women and wilt belie thyself more than thou dost women, and art every way a 920 base deceiver of women. And would deceive me too, would you?

FREEMAN.

Nay, faith, widow, this is judging without seeing the evidence.

WIDOW.

I say, you are a worn-out whoremaster at five and twenty 925 both in body and fortune, and cannot be trusted by the common wenches of the town, lest you should not pay them, nor by the wives of the town, lest you should pay them. So you want women and would have me your bawd, to procure them for you. 930

918. foulmouthed]   *Q1-2*;   foul-   919. wilt] *Q1-3*; will *Q4-8, O.*
mouth *Q3-8, O.*

915. *nick*] gamble.

FREEMAN.

    Faith, if you had any good acquaintance, widow, 'twould be civily done of thee, for I am just come from sea.

WIDOW.

    I mean, you would have me keep you that you might turn keeper, for poor widows are only used like bawds by you. You go to church with us but to get other women to lie 935 with. In fine, you are a cheating, chousing spendthrift, and, having sold your own annuity, would waste my jointure.

JERRY.

    And make havoc of our estate personal and all our old gilt plate. I should soon be picking up all our mortgaged 940 apostle spoons, bowls, and beakers out of most of the ale-houses betwixt Hercules Pillars and the Boatswain in Wapping. Nay, and you'd be scouring amongst my trees and make them knock down one another, like routed, reeling watchmen at midnight. Would you so, bully?   945

FREEMAN.

    Nay, prithee, widow, hear me.

WIDOW.

    No, sir. I'd have you to know, thou pitiful, paltry, lath-backed fellow, if I would have married a young man, 'tis well known I could have had any young heir in Norfolk, nay, the hopefulest young man this day at the Kings-Bench 950 Bar, I that am a relict and executrix of known plentiful assets and parts, who understand myself and the law. And would you have me under covert baron again? No, sir, no covert baron for me.

FREEMAN.

    But, dear widow, hear me. I value you only, not your 955 jointure.

WIDOW.

    Nay, sir, hold there. I know your love to a widow is covetousness of her jointure. And a widow a little stricken in years with a good jointure is like an old mansion house

---

941. *apostle spoons*] spoons with figures of the apostles for handles.
942–943. *betwixt . . . Wapping*] the whole length of London.
953. *under covert baron*] under a husband's protection—and control.

in a good purchase, never valued; but take one, take 960
t'other. And perhaps when you are in possession you'd
neglect it, let it drop to the ground for want of necessary
repairs or expenses upon it.

FREEMAN.

No, widow, one would be sure to keep all tight when one
is to forfeit one's lease by dilapidation.   965

WIDOW.

Fie, fie, I neglect my business with this foolish discourse
of love. Jerry, child, let me see the list of the jury. I'm sure
my cousin Olivia has some relations amongst them. But
where is she?

FREEMAN.

Nay, widow, but hear me one word only.   970

WIDOW.

Nay, sir, no more, pray. I will no more hearken again to
your foolish love motions than to offers of arbitration.

                        Exeunt Widow *and* Jerry.

FREEMAN.

Well, I'll follow thee yet, for he that has a pretension at
court or to a widow must never give over for a little ill
usage.   975

OLDFOX.

Therefore I'll get her by assiduity, patience, and long-
sufferings, which you will not undergo, for you idle young
fellows leave off love when it comes to be business, and
industry gets more women, than love.

FREEMAN.

Ay, industry, the fool's and old man's merit; but I'll be 980
industrious too and make a business on it and get her by
law, wrangling, and contests and not by sufferings. And,
because you are no dangerous rival, I'll give thee counsel,
major.

    If you litigious widow e'er would gain,   985
    Sigh not to her, but by the law complain:
    To her, as to a bawd, defendant sue
    With statutes, and make justice pimp for you.

                              Exeunt.

Finis actus secundi

ACT III

Westminster Hall.
Enter Manly *and* Freeman, *two* Sailors *behind.*

MANLY.

I hate this place, worse than a man that has inherited a chancery suit. I wish I were well out on it again.

FREEMAN.

Why, you need not be afraid of this place, for a man without money needs no more fear a crowd of lawyers than a crowd of pickpockets.   5

MANLY.

This, the reverend of the law would have thought the palace or residence of justice; but, if it be, she lives here with the state of a Turkish emperor, rarely seen, and besieged, rather than defended, by her numerous black guard here.   10

FREEMAN.

Methinks 'tis like one of their own halls in Christmas time, whither from all parts fools bring their money to try by the dice—not the worst judges—whether it shall be their own or no. But after a tedious fretting and wrangling they drop away all their money on both sides, and, finding neither   15 the better, at last go emptily and lovingly away together to the tavern, joining their curses against the young lawyers' box, that sweeps all like the old ones.

MANLY.

Spoken like a reveling Christmas lawyer.

FREEMAN.

Yes, I was one, I confess, but was fain to leave the law out 20 of conscience and fall to making false musters, rather chose to cheat the king than his subjects, plunder rather than take fees.

MANLY.

Well, a plague and a purse famine light on the law, and that female limb of it who dragged me hither today. But prithee 25 go see if in that crowd of daggled gowns there thou canst find her.

Pointing to a crowd of lawyers at the end of the stage.

Exit Freeman. *Manet* Manly.

How hard it is to be an hypocrite!
At least to me, who am but newly so.
I thought it once a kind of knavery,   30
Nay, cowardice, to hide one's faults; but now
The common frailty, love, becomes my shame.
He must not know I love th'ungrateful still,
Lest he contemn me more than she, for I,
It seems, can undergo a woman's scorn   35
But not a man's—

Enter to him Fidelia.

FIDELIA.
Sir, good sir, generous captain.
MANLY.
Prithee, kind impertinence, leave me. Why shouldst thou
follow me, flatter my generosity now, since thou know'st I
have no money left? If I had it, I'd give it thee, to buy my   40
quiet.
FIDELIA.
I never followed yet, sir, reward or fame but you alone, nor
do I now beg anything but leave to share your miseries. You
should not be a niggard of them, since methinks you have
enough to spare. Let me follow you now because you hate   45
me, as you have often said.
MANLY.
I ever hated a coward's company, I must confess.
FIDELIA.
Let me follow you till I am none then, for you, I'm sure,
will through such worlds of dangers that I shall be inured
to them. Nay, I shall be afraid of your anger more than   50
danger and so turn valiant out of fear. Dear captain, do not
cast me off till you have tried me once more. Do not, do not
go to sea again without me.
MANLY.
Thou to sea! To court, thou fool. Remember the advice I
gave thee: thou art a handsome spaniel and canst fawn   55
naturally. Go, busk about and run thyself into the next
great man's lobby. First fawn upon the slaves without and
then run into the lady's bedchamber. Thou may'st be
admitted at last to tumble her bed. Go seek, I say, and lose

me, for I am not able to keep thee. I have not bread for   60
myself.

FIDELIA.

Therefore I will not go, because then I may help and serve
you.

MANLY.

Thou!

FIDELIA.

I warrant you, sir, for at worst I could beg or steal for you.   65

MANLY.

Nay, more bragging! Dost thou not know there's venturing
your life in stealing? Go, prithee, away. Thou art as hard
to shake off as that flattering effeminating mischief, love.

FIDELIA.

Love, did you name? Why, you are not so miserable as to be
yet in love, sure!   70

MANLY.

No, no, prithee away, be gone, or— (*Aside.*)   I had almost
discovered my love and shame. Well, if I had? That thing
could not think the worse of me—or if he did?—No—yes,
he shall know it—he shall—but then I must never leave him,
for they are such secrets that make parasites and pimps lords   75
of their masters. For any slavery or tyranny is easier than
love's.   [*Aloud.*]   Come hither. Since thou art so forward
to serve me, hast thou but resolution enough to endure the
torture of a secret? For such to some is insupportable.

FIDELIA.

I would keep it as safe as if your dear precious life depended   80
on it.

MANLY.

Damn your dearness. It concerns more than my life, my
honor.

FIDELIA.

Doubt it not, sir.

MANLY.

And do not discover it by too much fear of discovering it,   85
but have a great care you let not Freeman find it out.

FIDELIA.

I warrant you, sir. I am already all joy with the hopes of

your commands, and shall be all wings in the execution of them. Speak quickly, sir.

MANLY.

You said you would beg for me.   90

FIDELIA.

I did, sir.

MANLY.

Then you shall beg for me.

FIDELIA.

With all my heart, sir.

MANLY.

That is, pimp for me.

FIDELIA.

How, sir?   95

MANLY.

D'ye start! Thinkst thou thou couldst do me any other service? Come, no dissembling honor. I know you can do it handsomely. Thou wert made for it. You have lost your time with me at sea. You must recover it.

FIDELIA.

Do not, sir, beget yourself more reasons for your aversion to 100 me and make my obedience to you a fault. I am the unfittest in the world to do you such a service.

MANLY.

Your cunning arguing against it shows but how fit you are for it. No more dissembling. Here, I say, you must go use it for me to Olivia.   105

FIDELIA.

To her, sir?

MANLY.

Go flatter, lie, kneel, promise, anything to get her for me. I cannot live unless I have her. Didst thou not say thou wouldst do anything to save my life? And she said you had a persuading face.   110

FIDELIA.

But did not you say, sir, your honor was dearer to you than your life? And would you have me contribute to the loss of

---

89. quickly, sir] *Q1–2*; quickly,   111. not you] *Q1–6, Q8, O*; you
Q3; quickly. *Q4–8*; quickly, sir, *O.*   not *Q7.*

that and carry love from you to the most infamous, most false, and—

MANLY.

And most beautiful! *Sighs aside.* 115

FIDELIA.

Most ungrateful woman that ever lived, for sure she must be so that could desert you so soon, use you so basely, and so lately too. Do not, do not forget it, sir, and think—

MANLY.

No, I will not forget it but think of revenge. I will lie with her, out of revenge. Go, be gone, and prevail for me or 120 never see me more.

FIDELIA.

You scorned her last night.

MANLY.

I know not what I did last night. I dissembled last night.

FIDELIA.

Heavens!

MANLY.

Be gone, I say, and bring me love or compliance back, or 125 hopes at least, or I'll never see thy face again. By—

FIDELIA.

O do not swear, sir. First hear me.

MANLY.

I am impatient. Away. You'll find me here till twelve.

Turns away.

FIDELIA.

Sir—

MANLY.

Not one word, no insinuating argument more, or soothing 130 persuasion. You'll have need of all your rhetoric with her. Go, strive to alter her, not me. Be gone.

Exit Manly *at the end of the stage. Manet* Fidelia.

FIDELIA.

Should I discover to him now my sex,
And lay before him his strange cruelty,
'Twould but incense it more. —No, 'tis not time. 135
For his love, must I then betray my own?
Were ever love or chance, till now, severe?
Or shifting woman posed with such a task?

Forced to beg that which kills her if obtained,
And give away her lover not to lose him.   140

Exit Fidelia.

Enter Widow Blackacre *in the middle of half a dozen lawyers, whispered
to by a fellow in black,* Jerry Blackacre *following the crowd.*

WIDOW.

Offer me a reference, you saucy companion you! D'ye know
who you speak to? Art thou a solicitor in chancery and offer
a reference? A pretty fellow! Mr. Sergeant Ploddon, here's
a fellow has the impudence to offer me a reference.

SERGEANT PLODDON.

Who's that has the impudence to offer a reference within 145
these walls?

WIDOW.

Nay, for a splitter of causes to do it!

SERGEANT PLODDON.

No, madam, to a lady learned in the law as you are the
offer of a reference were to impose upon you.

WIDOW.

No, no, never fear me for a reference, Mr. Sergeant. But, 150
come, have you not forgot your brief? Are you sure you
shan't make the mistake of—hark you— (*Whispers.*) Go
then, go to your Court of Common Pleas, and say one thing
over and over again. You do it so naturally, you'll never be
suspected for protracting time.   155

SERGEANT PLODDON.

Come, I know the course of the court, and your business.

Exit Sergeant Ploddon.

WIDOW.

Let's see, Jerry, where are my minutes? Come, Mr. Quaint,
pray, go talk a great deal for me in chancery. Let your
words be easy, and your sense hard. My cause requires it.
Branch it bravely and deck my cause with flowers that the 160
snake may lie hidden. Go, go, and be sure you remember

158. in] *Q 1–4, Q 8, O*; in the *Q 5–7.*

---

141. *reference*] composition outside court.

the decree of my Lord Chancellor *tricesimo quart'* of the
Queen.

QUAINT.

I will, as I see cause, extenuate, or amplify matter of fact,
baffle truth with impudence, answer exceptions with ques-   165
tions, though never so impertinent, for reasons give them
words, for law and equity, tropes and figures. And so relax
and enervate the sinews of their argument with the oil of
my eloquence. But when my lungs can reason no longer,
and not being able to say anything more for our cause, say   170
everything of our adversary, whose reputation, though
never so clear and evident in the eye of the world, yet with
sharp invectives—

WIDOW.

(Alias Billingsgate.)

QUAINT.

With poignant and sour invectives, I say, I will deface,   175
wipe out, and obliterate his fair reputation, even as a record
with the juice of lemons, and tell such a story—for the truth
on it is all that we can do for our client in chancery is telling
a story—a fine story, a long story, such a story—

WIDOW.

Go, save thy breath for the cause. Talk at the bar, Mr.   180
Quaint. You are so copiously fluent you can weary anyone's
ears sooner than your own tongue. Go, weary our
adversary's counsel and the court. Go, thou art a fine-spoken
person. Adad, I shall make thy wife jealous of me if you
can but court the court into a decree for us. Go, get you   185
gone, and remember— (*Whispers.*)   *Exit* Quaint.
Come, Mr. Blunder, pray bawl soundly for me at the Kings
Bench, bluster, sputter, question, cavil, but be sure your
argument be intricate enough to confound the court, and
then you do my business. Talk what you will but be sure   190

164. amplify] *Q2–8*; examplifie *Q1*,   187. bawl] *Q1–3, Q5–7, O*; haul
O.   *Q4, Q8*.
186. and] *Q1, O*; *om. Q2–8*.

162. *tricesimo quart'*] The thirty-fourth year of an English queen would
have to be 1592.

your tongue never stand still, for your own noise will secure
your sense from censure. 'Tis like coughing or hemming
when one has got the bellyache, which stifles the unmannerly noise. Go, dear rogue, and succeed and I'll invite thee
ere it be long to more soused venison.   195

BLUNDER.

I'll warrant you, after your verdict your judgment shall not
be arrested upon if's and and's.   [*Exit* Blunder.]

WIDOW.

Come, Mr. Petulant, let me give you some new instructions
for our cause in the Exchequer. Are the barons sate?

PETULANT.

Yes, no. May be they are, may be they are not. What know 200
I? What care I?

WIDOW.

Hey day! I wish you would but snap up the counsel on
t'other side anon, at the bar, as much. And have a little
more patience with me that I might instruct you a little
better.   205

PETULANT.

You instruct me! What is my brief for, mistress?

WIDOW.

Ay, but you seldom read your brief but at the bar, if you
do it then.

PETULANT.

Perhaps I do, perhaps I don't, and perhaps 'tis time
enough. Pray hold yourself contented, mistress.   210

WIDOW.

Nay, if you go there too, I will not be contented, sir.
Though you, I see, will lose my cause for want of speaking,
I won't. You shall hear me and shall be instructed. Let's
see your brief.

PETULANT.

Send your solicitor to me. Instructed by a woman! I'd have 215
you to know, I do not wear a bar-gown—

WIDOW.

By a woman! And I'd have you to know, I am no common
woman but a woman conversant in the laws of the land, as
well as yourself, though I have no bar-gown.

PETULANT.

Go to, go to, mistress. You are impertinent, and there's your 220
brief for you. Instruct me!

Flings her breviate at her.

WIDOW.

Impertinent to me, you saucy Jack you! You return my
breviate but where's my fee? You'll be sure to keep that and
scan that so well that if there chance to be but a brass half-
crown in it, one's sure to hear on't again. Would you would 225
but look on your breviate half so narrowly. But pray give
me my fee too as well as my brief.

PETULANT.

Mistress, that's without precedent. When did a counsel ever
return his fee, pray? And you are impertinent, and ignorant,
to demand it.   230

WIDOW.

Impertinent again and ignorant to me! Gadsbodikins, you
puny upstart in the law, to use me so, you green bag carrier,
you murderer of unfortunate causes. The clerk's ink is
scarce off of your fingers, you that newly come from lamb-
lacking the judge's shoes and are not fit to wipe mine. You 235
call me impertinent and ignorant! I would give thee a cuff
on the ear, sitting the courts, if I were ignorant. Marry gep,
if it had not been for me, thou hadst been yet but a hearing
counsel at the bar.   *Exit* Petulant.

Enter Mr. Buttongown *crossing the stage in haste.*

Mr. Buttongown, Mr. Buttongown, whither so fast? What, 240
won't you stay till we are heard?

BUTTONGOWN.

I cannot, Mrs. Blackacre, I must be at the council. My
lord's cause stays there for me.

WIDOW.

And mine suffers here.

232. the] *Q1–6, Q8, O; om. Q7.*

---

237. *sitting the courts*] Violence while the court was in session drew extra
severity.

237. *Marry gep*] The *OED* derives this from "By Mary Gipcey, i.e., By
St. Mary of Egypt."

BUTTONGOWN.

I cannot help it.   245

WIDOW.

I'm undone.

BUTTONGOWN.

What's that to me?

WIDOW.

Consider the five pound fee if not my cause. That was something to you.

BUTTONGOWN.

Away, away, pray be not so troublesome, mistress. I must 250 be gone.

WIDOW.

Nay, but consider a little. I am your old client, my lord but a new one; or, let him be what he will, he will hardly be a better client to you than myself. I hope you believe I shall be in law as long as I live, therefore am no despicable client. 255 Well, but go to your lord. I know you expect he should make you a judge one day; but I hope his promise to you will prove a true lord's promise. But that he might be sure to fail you I wish you had his bond for it.

BUTTONGOWN.

But—what? Will you yet be thus impertinent, mistress?   260

WIDOW.

Nay, I beseech you, sir, stay, if it be but to tell me my lord's case. Come, in short.

BUTTONGOWN.

Nay then—   *Exit* Buttowngown.

WIDOW.

Well, Jerry, observe, child, and lay it up for hereafter: these are those lawyers who by being in all causes are in 265 none; therefore if you would have them for you, let your adversary fee them, for he may chance to depend upon them, and so in being against thee they'll be for thee.

JERRY.

Ay, mother, they put me in mind of the unconscionable wooers of widows, who undertake briskly their matrimonial 270 business for their money, but when they have got it once, let who will drudge for them. Therefore have a care of them, forsooth. There's advice for your advice.

WIDOW.

Well said, boy. Come, Mr. Splitcause, pray go see when
my cause in Chancery comes on; and go speak with Mr. 275
Quillet in the King's Bench and Mr. Quirk in the Common
Pleas and see how our matters go there.

Enter Major Oldfox.

OLDFOX.

Lady, a good and propitious morning to you, and may
all your causes go as well as if I myself were judge of them.

WIDOW.

Sir, excuse me, I am busy and cannot answer compliments 280
in Westminster Hall. Go, Mr. Splitcause, and come to me
again to that bookseller's. There I'll stay for you that you
may be sure to find me.

OLDFOX.

No, sir, come to the other bookseller's, I'll attend your
ladyship thither.   *Exit* Splitcause. 285

WIDOW.

Why to the other?

OLDFOX.

Because he is my bookseller, lady.

WIDOW.

What, to sell you lozenges for your catarrh? Or medicines
for your corns? What else can a major deal with a bookseller for?   290

OLDFOX.

Lady, he prints for me.

WIDOW.

Why, are you an author?

OLDFOX.

Of some few essays. Deign you, lady, to peruse them.
(*Aside.*) She is a woman of parts and I must win her by
showing mine.   295

The *Bookseller's* Boy.

BOY.

Will you see Culpepper, mistress? Aristotle's *Problems*? *The
Compleat Midwife*?

296–297. *Culpepper . . . Midwife*] The boy recommends household medical
guides; the widow wants law books (l. 298); Jerry's taste runs to adventure
(ll. 308–309).

WIDOW.

No, let's see Dalton, Hughs, Shepherd, Wingate.

BOY.

We have no lawbooks.

WIDOW.

No? You are a pretty bookseller then.   300

OLDFOX.

Come, have you e'er a one of my essays left?

BOY.

Yes, sir, we have enough, and shall always have them.

OLDFOX.

How so?

BOY.

Why, they are good, steady, lasting ware.

OLDFOX.

Nay, I hope they will live. Let's see. Be pleased, madam, 305
to peruse the poor endeavors of my pen, for I have a pen,
though I say it, that—   *Gives her a book.*

JERRY.

Pray let me see *St. George for Christendom* or *The Seven Champions of England.*

WIDOW.

No, no, give him *The Young Clerk's Guide.* What, we shall 310
have you read yourself into a humor of rambling, and
fighting, and studying military discipline and wearing red
breeches!

OLDFOX.

Nay, if you talk of military discipline, show him my treatise
of *The Art Military.*   315

WIDOW.

Hold, I would as willingly he should read a play.

JERRY.

O pray, forsooth, mother, let me have a play.

WIDOW.

No, sirrah, there are young students of the law enough
spoiled already by plays; they would make you in love with
your laundress or, what's worse, some queen of the stage 320

306. for . . . pen] *Q1, O*; *om. Q2–8.   Military Q2–8.
315. *Art Military*] *Q1, O*; *Art of*

that was a laundress, and so turn keeper before you are of
age.

Several crossing the stage.

But stay, Jerry, is not that Mr. What-d'y'call-him that goes
there, he that offered to sell me a suit in chancery for five
hundred pound, for a hundred down and only paying the 325
clerk's fees?

JERRY.

Ay, forsooth, 'tis he.

WIDOW.

Then stay here, and have a care of the bags whilst I
follow him. Have a care of the bags, I say.

JERRY.

And do you have a care, forsooth, of the statute against 330
champertee, I say.   *Exit* Widow.

Enter Freeman *to them.*

FREEMAN (*aside*).

So, there's a limb of my widow which was wont to be in-
separable from her. She can't be far. —How now, my
pretty son-in-law that shall be, where's my widow?

JERRY.

My mother, but not your widow, will be forthcoming 335
presently.

FREEMAN.

Your servant, major. What, are you buying furniture for a
little sleeping closet which you miscall a study? For you do
only by your books as by your wenches, bind them up neatly
and make them fine, for other people to use them: and 340
your bookseller is properly your upholster, for he furnishes
your room rather than your head.

OLDFOX.

Well, well, good sea lieutenant, study you your compass.
That's more than your head can deal with. (*Aside.*)   I
will go find out the widow to keep her out of his sight, or he'll 345
board her whilst I am treating a peace.

                    Exit Oldfox. *Manent* Freeman, Jerry.

---

331. *champertee*] champerty, a form of legal grubstaking.

JERRY.

Nay prithee, friend, now let me have but the *Seven Champions*. You shall trust me no longer than till my mother's Mr. Splitcause comes, for I hope he'll lend me wherewithal to pay for it.   350

FREEMAN.

Lend thee! Here, I'll pay him. Do you want money, squire? I'm sorry a man of your estate should want money.

JERRY.

Nay, my mother will ne'er let me be at age. And till then she says—

FREEMAN.

At age! Why, you are at age already to have spent an 355 estate, man; there are younger than you have kept their women these three years, have had half a dozen claps, and lost as many thousand pounds at play.

JERRY.

Ay, they are happy sparks! Nay, I know some of my schoolfellows who when we were at school were two years younger 360 than me but now, I know not how, are grown men before me and go where they will and look to themselves, but my curmudgeonly mother won't allow me wherewithal to be a man of myself with.

FREEMAN.

Why there 'tis. I knew your mother was in the fault. Ask 365 but your schoolfellows what they did to be men of themselves.

JERRY.

Why, I know they went to law with their mothers, for they say there's no good to be done upon a widow mother till one goes to law with her, but mine is as plaguey a lawyer as any 370 of our inn. Then would she marry too and cut down my trees. Now I should hate, man, to have my father's wife kissed, and slapped, and t'other thing too (you know what I mean) by another man, and our trees are the purest, tall, even, shady twigs, by my fa—   375

FREEMAN.

Come, squire, let your mother and your trees fall as she pleases rather than wear this gown and carry green bags all

thy life, and be pointed at for a tony. But you shall be able
to deal with her yet the common way; thou shalt make false
love to some lawyer's daughter, whose father, upon the 380
hopes of thy marrying her, shall lend thee money, and law,
to preserve thy estate and trees, and thy mother is so ugly
nobody will have her if she cannot cut down thy trees.

JERRY.

Nay, if I had but anybody to stand by me, I am as stomachful as another.   385

FREEMAN.

That will I. I'll not see any hopeful young gentleman
abused.

BOY (aside).

By any but yourself.

JERRY.

The truth on't is, mine's as arrant a widow-mother to her
poor child as any in England. She won't so much as let one 390
have sixpence in one's pocket to see a motion or the dancing
of the ropes or—

FREEMAN.

Come, you shan't want money. There's gold for you.

JERRY.

O Lord, sir, two guineas! D'ye lend me this? Is there no
trick in it? Well, sir, I'll give you my bond for security. 395

FREEMAN.

No, no, thou hast given me thy face for security. Anybody
would swear thou dost not look like a cheat. You shall have
what you will of me, and if your mother will not be kinder
to you, come to me, who will.

JERRY (aside).

By my fa—he's a curious fine gentleman!— [Aloud.]   But, 400
will you stand by one?

388. any] Q 1–4, Q 8, O; any other
Q 5–7.

---

378. *tony*] simpleton.
384–385. *stomachful*] slightly more elegant equivalent of our modern term
for having courage.

FREEMAN.

If you can be resolute.

JERRY.

Can be resolved! Gad, if she gives me but a cross word, I'll leave her tonight and come to you. But now I have got money I'll go to Jack of All Trades, at t'other end of the 405 Hall, and buy the neatest, purest things—

FREEMAN [*aside.*]

And I'll follow the great boy and my blow at his mother. Steal away the calf and the cow will follow you.

Exit Jerry, *followed by* Freeman.

Enter, on the other side, Manly, Widow Blackacre, *and* Oldfox.

MANLY.

Damn your cause. Can't you lose it without me? Which you are like enough to do if it be, as you say, an honest one. 410 I will suffer no longer for it.

WIDOW.

Nay, captain, I tell you, you are my prime witness and the cause is just now coming on, Mr. Splitcause tells me. Lord, methinks you should take a pleasure in walking here as half you see now do, for they have no business here, I assure you. 415

MANLY.

Yes, but I'll assure you then, their business is to persecute me, but d'ye think I'll stay any longer, to have a rogue, because he knows my name, pluck me aside and whisper a newsbook-secret to me with a stinking breath? A second come piping angry from the court and sputter in my face his 420 tedious complaints against it? A third law-coxcomb, because he saw me once at a reader's dinner, come and put me a long law case, to make a discovery of his indefatigable dullness and my wearied patience? A fourth, a most barbarous civil rogue, who will keep a man half an hour in the 425 crowd with a bowed body and a hat off, acting the reformed sign of the Salutation Tavern, to hear his bountiful professions of service and friendship, whilst he cares not if I were

---

419. *newsbook-secret*] common knowledge from being published in the papers.

422. *reader's dinner*] banquet by, and for, honorary lecturers in law.

damned and I am wishing him hanged out of my way? I'd
as soon run the gauntlet as walk t'other turn.   430

Enter to them Jerry Blackacre *without his bags, but laden with trinkets,
which he endeavors to hide from his mother, and followed at a distance by*
Freeman.

WIDOW.

 O, are you come, sir? But where have you been, you ass?
And how come you thus laden?

JERRY.

 Look here, forsooth mother, now here's a duck, here's a
boar-cat, and here's an owl.
   Making a noise with catcalls and other such like instruments.

WIDOW.

 Yes, there is an owl, sir.   435

OLDFOX.

 He's an ungracious bird, indeed.

WIDOW.

 But go, thou trangame, and carry back those trangames
which thou hast stolen or purloined, for nobody would
trust a minor in Westminster Hall sure.

JERRY.

 Hold yourself contented, forsooth. I have these commodities 440
by a fair bargain and sale, and there stands my witness and
creditor.

WIDOW.

 How's that! What, sir, d'ye think to get the mother by
giving the child a rattle? But where are my bags, my
writings, you rascal?   445

JERRY (*aside*).

 O law! Where are they indeed?

WIDOW.

 How, sirrah? Speak, come—

MANLY (*apart to him*).

 You can tell her, Freeman, I suppose?

FREEMAN (*apart to him*).

 'Tis true, I made one of your salt-water sharks steal them,

448. You] *Q1–3, O;* Who *Q4–8.*

whilst he was eagerly choosing his commodities, as he calls   450
them, in order to my design upon his mother.

WIDOW.

Won't you speak? Where were you, I say, you son of a—an
unfortunate woman? O major, I'm undone. They are all
that concern my estate, my jointure, my husband's deed of
gift, my evidences for all my suits now depending! What   455
will become of them?

FREEMAN (*aside*).

I'm glad to hear this. —They'll be safe, I warrant you,
madam.

WIDOW.

O where? Where? Come, you villain, along with me and
show me where.   460

       Exeunt Widow, Jerry, Oldfox. *Manent* Manly, Freeman.

MANLY.

Thou hast taken the right way to get a widow, by making
her great boy rebel, for when nothing will make a widow
marry she'll do it to cross her children. But canst thou in
earnest marry this harpy, this volume of shriveled, blurred
parchments and law, this attorney's desk?   465

FREEMAN.

Ay, ay, I'll marry and live honestly, that is, give my creditors, not her, due benevolence, pay my debts.

MANLY.

Thy creditors, you see, are not so barbarous as to put thee
in prison, and wilt thou commit thyself to a noisome dun-
geon for thy life, which is the only satisfaction thou canst   470
give thy creditors by this match?

FREEMAN.

Why, is not she rich?

MANLY.

Ay, but he that marries a widow for her money will find
himself as much mistaken as the widow that marries a
young fellow for due benevolence, as you call it.   475

FREEMAN.

Why, d'ye think I shan't deserve wages? I'll drudge faithfully.

457. safe] *Q1, Q3–8, O*; save *Q2.*

MANLY.

I tell thee again, he that is the slave in the mine has the
least propriety in the ore. You may dig and dig, but if thou
wouldst have her money rather get to be her trustee than 480
her husband, for a true widow will make over her estate to
anybody and cheat herself rather than be cheated by her
children or a second husband.

Enter to them Jerry, *running in a fright.*

JERRY.

O law! I'm undone, I'm undone. My mother will kill me.
You said you'd stand by one.   485

FREEMAN.

So I will, my brave squire, I warrant thee.

JERRY.

Ay, but I dare not stay till she comes, for she's as furious,
now she has lost her writings, as a bitch when she has lost
her puppies.

MANLY.   490
The comparison's handsome!

JERRY.

O, she's here!

Enter Widow Blackacre *and* Oldfox.

FREEMAN (*to the* Sailor).

Take him, Jack, and make haste with him to your master's
lodging, and be sure you keep him up till I come.
                                    Exeunt Jerry *and* Sailor.

WIDOW.

O my dear writings! Where's this heathen rogue, my
minor?   495

FREEMAN.

Gone to drown or hang himself.

WIDOW.

No, I know him too well, he'll ne'er be *felo de se* that way;

491. here] *Q1–4, Q8, O;* there   493.1. *Exeunt*] *Exit Q1–3; Ex.*
Q5–7.   *Q4–8, O.*

but he may go and choose a guardian of his own head and
so be *felo de ses biens*: for he has not yet chosen one.

FREEMAN (*aside*).

Say you so? And he shan't want one.   500

WIDOW.

But, now I think on't, 'tis you, sir, have put this cheat upon
me; for there is a saying, take hold of a maid by her smock,
and a widow by her writings, and they cannot get from you.
But I'll play fast and loose with you yet, if there be law, and
my minor and writings are not forthcoming, I'll bring my 505
action of detinue or trover. But first I'll try to find out this
guardianless, graceless villain. Will you jog, major?

MANLY.

If you have lost your evidence, I hope your causes cannot
go on, and I may be gone?

WIDOW.

O no, stay but a making-water while, as one may say, and 510
I'll be with you again.

Exeunt Widow and Oldfox. *Manent* Manly, Freeman.

FREEMAN.

Well, sure I am the first man that ever began a love
intrigue in Westminster Hall.

MANLY.

No, sure, for the love to a widow generally begins here. And
as the widow's cause goes against the heir or executors, the 515
jointure rivals commence their suit to the widow.

FREEMAN.

Well, but how, pray, have you passed your time here since I
was forced to leave you alone? You have had a great deal of
patience.

MANLY.

Is this a place to be alone or have patience in? But I have 520
had patience indeed, for I have drawn upon me, since I
came, but three quarrels, and two lawsuits.

499. *biens*] Q4–8; *beins* Q1–3, O.   511.1. *Manent*] Q1–7; *Manet* Q8,
511.1. *Exeunt*] Ex. Q1–7; Exit   O.
Q8, O.

499. *felo de ses biens*] murderer of his own property—by analogy with *felo
de se* (suicide).

FREEMAN.

Nay, faith, you are too cursed to be let loose in the world;
you should be tied up again in your sea kennel called a ship.
But how could you quarrel here? 525

MANLY.

How could I refrain? A lawyer talked peremptorily and
saucily to me and as good as gave me the lie.

FREEMAN.

They do it so often to one another at the bar that they make
no bones on it elsewhere.

MANLY.

However, I gave him a cuff on the ear; whereupon he jogs 530
two men, whose backs were turned to us, for they were reading at a bookseller's, to witness I struck him sitting the courts,
which office they so readily promised that I called them
rascals and knights of the post. One of them presently calls
two other absent witnesses who were coming toward us at a 535
distance, whilst the other with a whisper desires to know my
name that he might have satisfaction by way of challenge
as t'other by way of writ, but if it were not rather to direct
his brother's writ than his own challenge. There you see is
one of my quarrels and two of my lawsuits. 540

FREEMAN.

So—and the other two?

MANLY.

For advising a poet to leave off writing and turn lawyer
because he is dull and impudent and says or writes nothing
now but by precedent.

FREEMAN.

And the third quarrel? 545

MANLY.

For giving more sincere advice to a handsome, well-dressed
young fellow—who asked it too—not to marry a wench
that he loved and I had lain with.

FREEMAN.

Nay, if you will be giving your sincere advice to lovers and
poets you will not fail of quarrels. 550

539. is] *Q1-7, O; om. Q8.*

MANLY.

Or if I stay in this place, for I see more quarrels crowding upon me. Let's be gone and avoid them.

Enter Novel, *at a distance, coming towards them.*

A plague on him, that sneer is ominous to us; he is coming upon us and we shall not be rid of him.

NOVEL.

Dear bully, don't look so grum upon me; you told me just 555 now you had forgiven me a little harmless raillery upon wooden legs last night.

MANLY.

Yes, yes, pray be gone. I am talking of business.

NOVEL.

Can't I hear it? I love thee and will be faithful and always—

MANLY.

Impertinent! 'Tis business that concerns Freeman only. 560

NOVEL.

Well, I love Freeman too and would not divulge his secret. Prithee speak, prithee, I must—

MANLY.

Prithee let me be rid of thee. I must be rid of thee.

NOVEL.

Faith, thou canst hardly, I love thee so. Come, I must know the business. 565

MANLY (*aside*).

So, I have it now. —Why, if you needs will know it, he has a quarrel and his adversary bids him bring two friends with him. Now, I am one, and we are thinking who we shall have for a third.

Several crossing the stage.

NOVEL.

A pox, there goes a fellow owes me an hundred pound and 570 goes out of town tomorrow. I'll speak with him and come to you presently. *Exit* Novel.

MANLY.

No but you won't.

FREEMAN.

You are dextrously rid of him.

Enter Oldfox.

MANLY.

To what purpose, since here comes another as impertinent? 575
I know by his grin he is bound hither.

OLDFOX.

Your servant, worthy, noble captain. Well, I have left the
widow because she carried me from your company, for,
faith, captain, I must needs tell thee thou art the only
officer in England who was not an Edgehill officer that I 580
care for.

MANLY.

I'm sorry for it.

OLDFOX.

Why, wouldst thou have me love them?

MANLY.

Anybody rather than me.

OLDFOX.

What, you are modest I see! Therefore too I love thee.   585

MANLY.

No, I am not modest but love to brag myself and can't
patiently hear you fight over the last civil war; therefore go
look out the fellow I saw just now here, that walks with his
stockings and his sword out at heels, and let him tell you the
history of that scar on his cheek, to give you occasion to show 590
yours, got in the field at Bloomsbury, not that of Edgehill.
Go to him, poor fellow. He is fasting and has not yet the
happiness this morning to stink of brandy and tobacco. Go,
give him some to hear you. I am busy.

OLDFOX.

Well, ygad, I love thee now, boy, for thy surliness. Thou art 595
no tame captain, I see, that will suffer—

MANLY.

An old fox.

OLDFOX.

All that shan't make me angry. I consider thou art peevish

---

580. *Edgehill*] scene of battle in 1642.
591. *Bloomsbury*] in 1676, open fields at the edge of London and popular
duelling grounds.

and fretting at some ill success at law. Prithee tell me what
ill luck you have met with here.   600

MANLY.

You.

OLDFOX.

Do I look like the picture of ill luck? Gadsnouns, I love thee
more and more; and shall I tell thee what made me love
thee first?

MANLY.

Do, that I may be rid of that damned quality and thee.   605

OLDFOX.

'Twas thy wearing that broad sword there.

MANLY.

Here, Freeman, let's change. I'll never wear it more.

OLDFOX.

How! You won't sure. Prithee don't look like one of our
holiday captains nowadays, with a bodkin by your side,
your martinet rogues.   610

MANLY (*aside*).

O, then there's hopes. —What, d'ye find fault with martinet? Let me tell you, sir, 'tis the best exercise in the world,
the most ready, most easy, most graceful exercise that ever
was used and the most—

OLDFOX.

Nay, nay, sir, no more, sir, your servant. If you praise 615
martinet once, I have done with you, sir. Martinet!
Martinet!   *Exit* Oldfox.

FREEMAN.

Nay, you have made him leave you as willingly as ever he
did an enemy, for he was truly for the king and parliament.
For the parliament in their list, and for the king in cheating 620
them of their pay, and never hurting the king's party in the
field.

Enter a Lawyer *towards them.*

MANLY.

A pox! This way; here's a lawyer I know threatening us
with another greeting.

610. your martinet] *Q1–7*; you   616. sir. Martinet] *Q1–3, O*; Sir
martinet *Q8, O*.   Martinet *Q4–8*.

LAWYER.

    Sir, sir, your very servant. I was afraid you had forgotten 625
me.

MANLY.

    I was not afraid you had forgotten me.

LAWYER.

    No, sir, we lawyers have pretty good memories.

MANLY.

    You ought to have, by your wits.

LAWYER.

    O, you are a merry gentleman, sir. I remember you were 630
merry when I was last in your company.

MANLY.

    I was never merry in thy company, Mr. Lawyer, sure.

LAWYER.

    Why, I'm sure you joked upon me and shammed me all
night long.

MANLY.

    Shammed! Prithee what barbarous law term is that?   635

LAWYER.

    Shamming! Why, don't you know that? 'Tis all our way of
wit, sir.

MANLY.

    I am glad I do not know it then. Shamming! What does he
mean by it, Freeman?

FREEMAN.

    Shamming is telling you an insipid, dull lie, with a dull 640
face, which the sly wag the author only laughs at himself,
and making himself believe 'tis a good jest, puts the sham
only upon himself.

MANLY.

    So your lawyer's jest, I find, like his practice, has more
knavery than wit in it. I should make the worst shammer in 645
England. I must always deal ingenuously, as I will with you,
Mr. Lawyer, and advise you to be seen rather with attorneys
and solicitors than such fellows as I am; they will credit your
practice more.

646. ingenuously] *Q6–7*; ingeni-   646. as I will] *Q1–3*; as well *Q4–8,*
ously *Q1–5, 8, O.*   *O.*

LAWYER.

No, sir, your company's an honor to me.   650

MANLY.

No, faith, go this way, there goes an attorney. Leave me for
him. Let it be never said a lawyer's civility did him hurt.

LAWYER.

No, worthy, honored sir, I'll not leave you for any attorney
sure.

MANLY.

Unless he had a fee in his hand.   655

LAWYER.

Have you any business here, sir? Try me. I'd serve you
sooner than any attorney breathing.

MANLY.

Business!— (*Aside.*) So, I have thought of a sure way.
—Yes, faith, I have a little business.

LAWYER.

Have you so, sir? In what court, sir? What is it, sir? Tell 660
me but how I may serve you and I'll do it, sir, and take it
for as great an honor—

MANLY.

Faith, 'tis for a poor orphan of a sea officer of mine that has
no money; but if it could be followed *in forma pauperis*, and
when the legacy's recovered—   665

LAWYER.

Forma pauperis, sir!

MANLY.

Ay, sir.

Several crossing the stage.

LAWYER.

Mr. Bumblecase, Mr. Bumblecase, a word with you. —Sir,
I beg your pardon at present, I have a little business—

MANLY.

Which is not *in forma pauperis*.   *Exit* Lawyer. 670

FREEMAN.

So, you have now found a way to be rid of people without
quarreling.

---

664. *in forma pauperis*] The lawyer's service would be gratis for a pauper
client.

Enter Alderman.

MANLY.

But here's a city rogue will stick as hard upon us as if I owed
him money.

ALDERMAN.

Captain, noble sir, I am yours heartily d'ye see. Why 675
should you avoid your old friends?

MANLY.

And why should you follow me? I owe you nothing.

ALDERMAN.

Out of my hearty respects to you, for there is not a man in
England—

MANLY.

Thou wouldst save from hanging with the expense of a 680
shilling only.

ALDERMAN.

Nay, nay, but captain, you are like enough to tell me—

MANLY.

Truth, which you won't care to hear; therefore you had better go talk with somebody else.

ALDERMAN.

No, I know nobody can inform me better of some young wit 685
or spendthrift that has a good dipped seat and estate in
Middlesex, Hertfordshire, Essex, or Kent. Any of these
would serve my turn. Now, if you knew of such an one and
would but help—

MANLY.

You to finish his ruin.   690

ALDERMAN.

I'faith, you should have a snip—

MANLY.

Of your nose. You thirty in the hundred rascal, would you
make me your squire setter, your bawd for manors?

Takes him by the nose.

ALDERMAN.

Oh!

FREEMAN.

Hold or here will be your third lawsuit.   695

---

686. *dipped seat*] mortgaged country estate.

ALDERMAN.

Gad's precious, you hectoring person you, are you wild?
I meant you no hurt, sir. I begin to think, as things go, land
security best and have, for a convenient mortgage, some
ten, fifteen, or twenty thousand pound by me.

MANLY.

Then go lay it out upon a hospital and take a mortgage of 700
heaven according to your city custom, for you think by
laying out a little money to hook in that too hereafter. Do,
I say, and keep the poor you've made by taking for-
feitures that heaven may not take yours.

ALDERMAN.

No, to keep the cripples you make this war; this war spoils 705
our trade.

MANLY.

Damn your trade. 'Tis the better for it.

ALDERMAN.

What, will you speak against our trade?

MANLY.

And dare you speak against the war, our trade?

ALDERMAN (aside).

Well, he may be a convoy of ships I am concerned in. 710
—Come, captain, I will have a fair correspondency with
you, say what you will.

MANLY.

Then prithee be gone.

ALDERMAN.

No, faith, prithee, captain, let's go drink a dish of laced
coffee and talk of the times. Come, I'll treat you. Nay, you 715
shall go, for I have no business here.

MANLY.

But I have.

ALDERMAN.

To pick up a man to give thee a dinner? Come, I'll do thy
business for thee.

MANLY.

Faith, now I think on it, so you may as well as any man, for 720
'tis to pick up a man to be bound with me to one who
expects city security, for—

ALDERMAN.

Nay, then your servant, captain. Business must be done.

MANLY.

Ay, if it can, but hark you, alderman, without you—

ALDERMAN.

Business sir, I say, must be done, and there's an officer of 725
the treasury I have an affair with—

Several crossing the stage. Exit Alderman.

MANLY.

You see now what the mighty friendship of the world is,
what all ceremony, embraces, and plentiful professions come
to. You are no more to believe a professing friend than a
threatening enemy, and as no man hurts you that tells you 730
he'll do you a mischief, no man, you see, is your servant
who says he is so. Why, the devil, then should a man be
troubled with the flattery of knaves, if he be not a fool, or
cully, or with the fondness of fools, if he be not a knave or
cheat?   735

FREEMAN.

Only for his pleasure, for there is some in laughing at fools
and disappointing knaves.

MANLY.

That's a pleasure, I think, would cost you too dear, as well
as marrying your widow to disappoint her; but, for my part,
I have no pleasure by them, but in despising them, where- 740
soe'er I meet them, and then the pleasure of hoping so to be
rid of them. But now my comfort is, I am not worth a shilling in the world, which all the world shall know; and then
I'm sure I shall have none of them come near me.

FREEMAN.

A very pretty comfort, which I think you pay too dear for. 745
But is the twenty pound gone since the morning?

MANLY.

To my boat's crew. Would you have the poor, honest, brave
fellows want?

FREEMAN.

Rather than you or I.

MANLY.

Why, art thou without money? Thou who art a friend to 750
everybody?

FREEMAN.

I ventured my last stake upon the squire, to nick him of his
mother and cannot help you to a dinner, unless you will go
dine with my lord—

MANLY.

No, no, the ordinary is too dear for me, where flattery must 755
pay for my dinner. I am no herald, or poet.

FREEMAN.

We'll go then to the bishop's—

MANLY.

There you must flatter the old philosophy. I cannot
renounce my reason for a dinner.

FREEMAN.

Why, then let's go to your alderman's.   760

MANLY.

Hang him, rogue! That were not to dine, for he makes you
drunk with lees of sack before dinner to take away your
stomach and there you must call usury and extortion God's
blessings, or the honest turning of the penny. Hear him
brag of the leather breeches in which he trotted first to town, 765
and make a greater noise with his money in his parlor, than
his cashiers do in his countinghouse without hopes of borrowing a shilling.

FREEMAN.

Ay, a pox on't, 'tis like dining with the great gamesters, and
when they fall to their common dessert, see the heaps of gold 770
drawn on all hands, without going to twelve. Let us go to
my Lady Goodly's.

MANLY.

There to flatter her looks you must mistake her grand-
children for her own, praise her cook that she may rail at
him, and feed her dogs, not yourself.   775

FREEMAN.

What d'ye think of eating with your lawyer then?

761. you] *Q1–3, O*; us *Q4–8*.   772. Goodly's] *Q1–5, Q8, O*; God-
764. blessings] *Q1–3, O*; blessing   ly's *Q6–7*.
Q4–8.

---

771. *without . . . twelve*] The meaning of what appears to be gambler's
argot has been lost. The context suggests "without joining the game."

MANLY.

Eat with him! Damn him, to hear him employ his barbarous
eloquence in a reading upon the two and thirty good bits
in a shoulder of veal, and be forced yourself to praise the
cold bribe pie that stinks, and drink law French wine as 780
rough and harsh as his law French. A pox on him. I'd rather
dine in the Temple Rounds or Walks with the knights
without noses, or the knights of the post, who are honester
fellows and better company. But let us home and try our
fortune; for I'll stay no longer here, for your damned 785
widow.

FREEMAN.

Well, let us go home then, for I must go for my damned
widow, and look after my new damned charge. Three or
four hundred year ago a man might have dined in this hall.

MANLY.

But now, the lawyer only here is fed: 790
And, bullylike, by quarrels gets his bread.

Exeunt.

Finis actus tertii

787. let us go home] *Q1–2, O*; let   791.1. *Exeunt*] *Q1–2*; *om. Q3–8,*
us go come *Q3*; let us come *Q4,*   *O.*
Q8; let us, come *Q5–7.*

782–783. *knights without noses*] vandalized statues of the crusaders in
Temple Church.
789. *dined . . . hall*] Westminster Hall had been originally a banquet-
ing hall.

ACT IV

Manly's lodging.
Enter Manly *and* Fidelia.

MANLY.

Well, there's success in thy face. Hast thou prevailed, say?
FIDELIA.

As I could wish, sir.
MANLY.

So, I told thee what thou wert fit for, and thou wouldst not
believe me. Come, thank me for bringing thee acquainted
with thy genius. Well, thou hast mollified her heart for me?   5
FIDELIA.

No, sir, not so, but what's better.
MANLY.

How? What's better?
FIDELIA.

I shall harden your heart against her.
MANLY.

Have a care, sir. My heart is too much in earnest to be
fooled with and my desire at height and needs no delays to   10
incite it. What, you are too good a pimp already and know
how to endear pleasure by withholding it? But leave off
your page's bawdyhouse tricks, sir, and tell me, will she be
kind?
FIDELIA.

Kinder than you could wish, sir.   15
MANLY.

So then. Well, prithee what said she?
FIDELIA.

She said—
MANLY.

What? Thou'rt so tedious. Speak comfort to me. What?
FIDELIA.

That, of all things, you were her aversion.
MANLY.

How?   20

0.1. *lodging*] *Q1–2*; *lodgings Q3–8*,
O.

FIDELIA.

That she would sooner take a bedfellow out of an hospital
and diseases into her arms than you.

MANLY.

What?

FIDELIA.

That she would rather trust her honor with a dissolute,
debauched hector, nay worse, with a finical, baffled coward,   25
all over loathsome with affectation of the fine gentleman.

MANLY.

What's all this you say?

FIDELIA.

Nay, that my offers of your love to her were more offensive
than when parents woo their virgin daughters to the enjoy-
ment of riches only and that you were in all circumstances   30
as nauseous to her as a husband on compulsion.

MANLY.

Hold, I understand you not.

FIDELIA (*aside*).

So, 'twill work, I see.

MANLY.

Did not you tell me—

FIDELIA.

She called you ten thousand ruffians.   35

MANLY.

Hold, I say.

FIDELIA.

Brutes—

MANLY.

Hold.

FIDELIA.

Sea monsters—

MANLY.

Damn your intelligence. Hear me a little now.   40

FIDELIA.

Nay, surly coward she called you too.

MANLY.

Won't you hold yet? Hold, or—

34. not you] *Q1–3*; you not *Q4–8*,
O.

FIDELIA.

Nay, sir, pardon me. I could not but tell you she had the
baseness, the injustice, to call you coward, coward, coward,
sir.   45

MANLY.

Not yet?

FIDELIA.

I've done. Coward, sir.

MANLY.

Did not you say she was kinder than I could wish her?

FIDELIA.

Yes, sir.

MANLY.

How then?—O—I understand you now. At first she   50
appeared in rage and disdain, the truest sign of a coming
woman, but at last you prevailed, it seems, did you not?

FIDELIA.

Yes, sir.

MANLY.

So then, let's know that only. Come, prithee, without
delays. I'll kiss thee for that news beforehand.   55

FIDELIA (*aside*).

So, the kiss, I'm sure, is welcome to me, whatsoe'er the news
will be to you.

MANLY.

Come, speak, my dear volunteer.

FIDELIA (*aside*).

How welcome were that kind word too, if it were not for
another woman's sake!   60

MANLY.

What, won't you speak? You prevailed for me at last, you
say?

FIDELIA.

No, sir.

MANLY.

No more of your fooling, sir. It will not agree with my
impatience or temper.   65

FIDELIA.

Then, not to fool you, sir, I spoke to her for you but prevailed

for myself. She would not hear me when I spoke in your
behalf but bid me say what I would in my own, though she
gave me no occasion, she was so coming and so was kinder,
sir, than you could wish, which I was only afraid to let you   70
know without some warning.

MANLY.

How's this? Young man, you are of a lying age, but I must
hear you out, and if—

FIDELIA.

I would not abuse you and cannot wrong her by any report
of her, she is so wicked.   75

MANLY.

How, wicked? Had she the impudence, at the second sight
of you only—

FIDELIA.

Impudence, sir! O, she has impudence enough to put a
court out of countenance and debauch a stews.

MANLY.

Why, what said she?   80

FIDELIA.

Her tongue, I confess, was silent, but her speaking eyes
gloated such things, more immodest and lascivious than
ravishers can act or women under a confinement think.

MANLY.

I know there are whose eyes reflect more obscenity than the
glasses in alcoves, but there are others too who use a little art   85
with their looks to make them seem more beautiful, not
more loving, which vain young fellows like you are apt
to interpret in their own favor and to the lady's wrong.

FIDELIA.

Seldom, sir. Pray have you a care of gloating eyes, for he that
loves to gaze upon them will find at last a thousand fools   90
and cuckolds in them, instead of cupids.

MANLY.

Very well, sir. But, what, you had only eye-kindness from
Olivia?

67. spoke] *Q1–2, Q5–6, O*; spake   85. too] *Q1, O*; *om. Q2–8.*
Q3–4, Q8; speak *Q7.*

FIDELIA.

I tell you again, sir, no woman sticks there. Eye-promises of
love they only keep. Nay, they are contracts which make   95
you sure of them. In short, sir, she, seeing me with shame
and amazement dumb, unactive, and resistless, threw her
twisting arms about my neck and smothered me with a
thousand tasteless kisses. Believe me, sir, they were so to me.

MANLY.

Why did you not avoid them then?   100

FIDELIA.

I fenced with her eager arms as you did with the grapples
of the enemy's fireship and nothing but cutting them off
could have freed me.

MANLY.

Damned, damned woman, that could be so false and
infamous! And damned, damned heart of mine, that cannot 105
yet be false, though so infamous! What easy, tame, suffering,
trampled things does that little god of talking cowards make
of us! But—

FIDELIA (aside).

So! It works I find as I expected.

MANLY.

But she was false to me before. She told me so herself, and 110
yet I could not quite believe it. But she was, so that her
second falseness is a favor to me, not an injury, in revenging
me upon the man that wronged me first of her love. Her
love!—A whore's, a witch's love!—But, what, did she not
kiss well, sir? I'm sure I thought her lips—but I must not 115
think of them more—but yet they are such I could still kiss
—grow to—and then tear off with my teeth, grind them into
mammocks and spit them into her cuckold's face.

FIDELIA (aside).

Poor man, how uneasy he is! I have hardly the heart to give
him so much pain though withal I give him a cure and to 120
myself new life.

MANLY.

But, what, her kisses sure could not but warm you into
desire at last or a compliance with hers at least?

119. he is] Q1–3, O; is he Q4–8.

FIDELIA.

Nay, more, I confess—

MANLY.

What more? Speak.   125

FIDELIA.

All you could fear had passed between us, if I could have
been made to wrong you, sir, in that nature.

MANLY.

Could have been made! You lie, you did.

FIDELIA.

Indeed, sir, 'twas impossible for me. Besides, we were interrupted by a visit. But, I confess, she would not let me stir 130
till I promised to return to her again within this hour, as
soon as it should be dark, by which time she would dispose
of her visit and her servants and herself for my reception,
which I was fain to promise to get from her.

MANLY.

Ha!   135

FIDELIA.

But if ever I go near her again, may you, sir, think me as
false to you as she is, hate and renounce me, as you ought
to do her and I hope will do now.

MANLY.

Well, but now I think on't, you shall keep your word with
your lady. What, a young fellow and fail the first, nay, so 140
tempting an assignation!

FIDELIA.

How, sir?

MANLY.

I say you shall go to her when 'tis dark and shall not disappoint her.

FIDELIA.

I, sir! I should disappoint her more by going, for—   145

MANLY.

How so?

FIDELIA.

Her impudence and injustice to you will make me disappoint her love, loathe her.

MANLY.

Come, you have my leave and if you disgust her, I'll go with
you and act love whilst you shall talk it only.   150

FIDELIA.

You, sir! Nay, then I'll never go near her. You act love, sir!
You must but act it indeed after all I have said to you. Think
of your honor, sir. Love—

MANLY.

Well, call it revenge and that is honorable. I'll be revenged
on her and thou shalt be my second.   155

FIDELIA.

Not in a base action, sir, when you are your own enemy. O,
go not near her, sir, for heaven's sake. For your own think
not of it.

MANLY.

How concerned you are! I thought I should catch you.
What, you are my rival at last and are in love with her   160
yourself and have spoken ill of her out of your love to her,
not me, and therefore would not have me go to her!

FIDELIA.

Heaven witness for me, 'tis because I love you only I would
not have you go to her.

MANLY.

Come, come, the more I think on't, the more I'm satisfied 165
you do love her. Those kisses, young man, I knew were
irresistible. 'Tis certain.

FIDELIA.

There is nothing certain in the world, sir, but my truth and
your courage.

MANLY.

Your servant, sir. Besides, false and ungrateful as she has 170
been to me, and though I may believe her hatred to me as
great as you report it, yet I cannot think you are so soon
and at that rate beloved by her though you may endeavor
it.

FIDELIA.

Nay, if that be all and you doubt it still, sir, I will conduct 175
you to her and, unseen, your ears shall judge of her falseness and my truth to you, if that will satisfy you.

MANLY.

Yes, there is some satisfaction in being quite out of doubt.
Because 'tis that alone withholds us from the pleasure of
revenge.   180

FIDELIA.

Revenge! What revenge can you have, sir? Disdain is best
revenged by scorn, and faithless love by loving another and
making her happy with the other's losings, which, if I
might advise—

Enter Freeman.

MANLY.

Not a word more.   185

FREEMAN.

What, are you talking of love yet, captain? I thought you
had done with it.

MANLY.

Why, what did you hear me say?

FREEMAN.

Something imperfectly of love, I think.

MANLY.

I was only wondering why fools, rascals, and desertless   190
wretches should still have the better of men of merit with all
women, as much as with their own common mistress,
fortune!

FREEMAN.

Because most women, like fortune, are blind, seem to do all
things in jest, and take pleasure in extravagant actions. 195
Their love deserves neither thanks or blame, for they cannot
help it. 'Tis all sympathy. Therefore the noisy, the finical,
the talkative, the cowardly and effeminate have the better
of the brave, the reasonable, and man of honor, for they
have no more reason in their love or kindness than fortune 200
herself.

MANLY.

Yes, they have their reason. First, honor in a man they fear
too much to love, and sense in a lover upbraids their want
of it, and they hate anything that disturbs their admiration
of themselves; but they are of that vain number who had 205
rather show their false generosity in giving away profusely
to worthless flatterers than in paying just debts. And, in

182. by loving] *Q1, O*; by the   184. might] *Q1–2, O*; must *Q3–8*.
loving *Q2–8*.   201. herself] *Q1–3, O*; it self *Q4–8*.

—113—

short, all women, like fortune, as you say, and rewards are
lost by too much meriting.

FIDELIA.

All women, sir! Sure there are some who have no other 210
quarrel to a lover's merit but that it begets their despair of
him.

MANLY.

Thou art young enough to be credulous, but we—

Enter Sailor.

SAILOR.

Here are now below the scolding, daggled gentlewoman and
that Major Old—old—Fop, I think you call him.   215

FREEMAN.

Oldfox. Prithee bid them come up, with your leave, captain,
for now I can talk with her upon the square, if I shall not
disturb you.

MANLY.

No, for I'll be gone. Come, volunteer.

FREEMAN.

Nay, pray stay. The scene between us will not be so tedious 220
to you as you think. Besides, you shall see how I have rigged
my squire out with the remains of my shipwrecked ward-
robe. He is under your sea *valet de chambre*'s hands and by
this time dressed and will be worth your seeing. Stay and
I'll fetch my fool.   225

MANLY.

No, you know I cannot easily laugh; besides, my volunteer
and I have business abroad.

            Exeunt Manly, Fidelia *on one side*, Freeman *on t'other*.

        Enter Major Oldfox *and* Widow Blackacre.

WIDOW.

What, nobody here! Did not the fellow say he was within?

OLDFOX.

Yes, lady, and he may be perhaps a little busy at present,
but if you think the time long till he comes, (*unfolding papers*) 230
I'll read you here some of the fruits of my leisure, the over-

220. between] *Q1–3, O*; betwixt
Q4–8.

flowings of my fancy and pen. (*Aside.*) To value me
right, she must know my parts. —Come—

WIDOW.

No, no, I have reading work enough of my own in my bag,
I thank you.   235

OLDFOX.

I, law, madam, but here is a poem in blank verse which I
think a handsome declaration of one's passion.

WIDOW.

O! If you talk of declarations, I'll show you one of the
prettiest penned things which I mended too myself you must
know.   240

OLDFOX.

Nay, lady, if you have used yourself so much to the reading
of harsh law that you hate smooth poetry, here is a character
for you of—

WIDOW.

A character! Nay, then I'll show you my bill in chancery
here that gives you such a character of my adversary, makes   245
him as black—

OLDFOX.

Pshaw, away, away, lady. But if you think the character too
long, here is an epigram not above twenty lines, upon a
cruel lady who decreed her servant should hang himself to
demonstrate his passion.   250

WIDOW.

Decreed! If you talk of decreeing, I have such a decree here,
drawn by the finest clerk—

OLDFOX.

O lady, lady, all interruption and no sense between us as
if we were lawyers at the bar! But I had forgot, Apollo
and Littleton never lodge in a head together. If you   255
hate verses, I'll give you a cast of my politics in prose. 'Tis a
letter to a friend in the country, which is now the way of all
such sober, solid persons as myself, when they have a mind

247. OLDFOX] *Q1–3, Q5–7, O*;
WID. *Q4, Q8.*

255. *Littleton*] Before Blackstone, Coke and Littleton were the universal
authorities on law.

to publish their disgust to the times, though perhaps, between you and I, they have no friend in the country. And 260
sure a politic, serious person may as well have a feigned
friend in the country to write to as well as an idle poet a
feigned mistress to write to. And so here is my letter to a
friend, or no friend, in the country concerning the late
conjuncture of affairs in relation to coffeehouses, or the 26₵
coffeeman's case.

WIDOW.

Nay, if your letter have a case in it, 'tis something, but first
I'll read you a letter of mine to a friend in the country called
a letter of attorney.

Enter to them Freeman *and* Jerry Blackacre *in an old gaudy suit and red
breeches of* Freeman's.

OLDFOX *(aside)*.

What, interruption still? O the plague of interruption, 270
worse to an author than the plague of critics!

WIDOW.

What's this I see, Jerry Blackacre, my minor, in red
breeches! What, hast thou left the modest, seemly garb
of gown and cap for this? And have I lost all my good Inns
of Chancery breeding upon thee then? And thou wilt go 275
a-breeding thyself, from our Inn of Chancery and Westminster Hall, at coffeehouses and ordinaries, playhouses,
tennis courts, and bawdyhouses.

JERRY.

Ay, ay, what then? Perhaps I will, but what's that to you?
Here's my guardian and tutor now, forsooth, that I am out 280
of your huckster's hands.

WIDOW.

How? Thou hast not chosen him for thy guardian yet?

JERRY.

No, but he has chosen me for his charge and that's all one,
and I'll do anything he'll have me and go all the world over
with him, to ordinaries and bawdyhouses, or anywhere else. 285

270.S.D. *(aside)*.] *Q 1–2, O; om.*
Q 3–8.

WIDOW.

To ordinaries and bawdyhouses! Have a care, minor. Thou
wilt infeeble there thy estate and body. Do not go to ordinaries and bawdyhouses, good Jerry.

JERRY.

Why, how come you to know any ill by bawdyhouses? You
never had any hurt by them, had you, forsooth? Pray hold 290
yourself contented. If I do go where money and wenches are
to be had, you may thank yourself, for you used me so
unnaturally, you would never let me have a penny to go
abroad with, nor so much as come near the garret, where
your maidens lay. Nay, you would not so much as let me 295
play at hotcockles with them, nor have any recreation with
them, though one should have kissed you behind, you were
so unnatural a mother, so you were.

FREEMAN.

Ay, a very unnatural mother, faith, squire.

WIDOW.

But Jerry, consider thou art yet but a minor; however, if 300
thou wilt go home with me again and be a good child, thou
shalt see—

FREEMAN.

Madam, I must have a better care of my heir under age than
so. I would sooner trust him alone with a stale waiting-
woman and a parson than with his widow mother and her 305
lover or lawyer.

WIDOW.

Why, thou villain, part mother and minor! Rob me of my
child and my writings! But thou shalt find there's law, and
as in the case of ravishment of guard—Westminster the
second.   310

OLDFOX.

Young gentleman, squire, pray be ruled by your mother
and your friends.

JERRY.

Yes, I'll be ruled by my friends, therefore not by my mother,

---

309. *ravishment*] The Second Statute of Westminster, 1285, covered
abduction of wards.

so I won't. I'll choose him for my guardian till I am of age,
nay, maybe for as long as I live. 315

WIDOW.

Wilt thou so, thou wretch? And when thou'rt of age, thou
wilt sign, seal, and deliver too, wilt thou?

JERRY.

Yes, marry will I, if you go there too.

WIDOW.

O do not squeeze wax, son. Rather go to ordinaries and
bawdyhouses than squeeze wax. If thou dost that, farewell 320
the goodly manor of Blackacre with all its woods, under-
woods, and appurtenances whatever. O, O! *Weeps.*

FREEMAN.

Come, madam, in short, you see I am resolved to have a
share in the estate, yours or your son's. If I cannot get you,
I'll keep him, who is less coy you find. But if you would have 325
your son again, you must take me too. Peace or war?
Love or law? You see my hostage is in my hand. I'm in
possession.

WIDOW.

Nay, if one of us must be ruined, e'en, let it be him. By my
body, a good one! Did you ever know yet a widow marry 330
or not marry for the sake of her child? I'd have you to know,
sir, I shall be hard enough for you both yet without marrying
you if Jerry won't be ruled by me. What say you, booby,
will you be ruled? Speak.

JERRY.

Let one alone, can't you? 335

WIDOW.

Wilt thou choose him for guardian whom I refuse for
husband?

JERRY.

Ay, to choose, I thank you.

WIDOW.

And are all my hopes frustrated? Shall I never hear thee put
cases again to John the butler or our vicar? Never see thee 340
amble the circuit with the judges and hear thee in our town
hall louder than the crier?

322.S.D. *Weeps.*] *Q1–7, O; om. Q8.*

JERRY.

No, for I have taken my leave of lawyering and pettifogging.

WIDOW.

Pettifogging! Thou profane villain, hast thou so? Petti- 345
fogging!—Then you shall take your leave of me and your
estate too. Thou shalt be an alien to me and it forever.
Pettifogging!

JERRY.

O, but if you go there too, mother, we have the deeds and
settlements, I thank you. Would you cheat me of my 350
estate, ifac?

WIDOW.

No, no, I will not cheat your little brother Bob, for thou
wert not born in wedlock.

FREEMAN.

How's that?

JERRY.

How? What quirk has she got in her head now?   355

WIDOW.

I say thou canst not, shalt not inherit the Blackacres' estate.

JERRY.

Why? Why, forsooth? What d'ye mean, if you go there too?

WIDOW.

Thou art but my base child and according to the law canst
not inherit it. Nay, thou art not so much as bastard eigne.

JERRY.

What, what? Am I then the son of a whore, mother?   360

WIDOW.

The law says—

FREEMAN.

Madam, we know what the law says, but have a care what
you say. Do not let your passion to ruin your son ruin your
reputation.

WIDOW.

Hang reputation, sir. Am not I a widow? Have no husband 365
nor intend to have any. Nor would you, I suppose, now

349. go] Q1–3, O; be Q4–8.   357. too] Q2–8, O; to Q1.

359. *eigne*] *aîné*, first-born.

have me for a wife. So I think now I'm revenged on my son
and you, without marrying, as I told you.

FREEMAN.

But consider, madam.

JERRY.

What, have you no shame left in you, mother?   370

WIDOW (*aside to* Oldfox).

Wonder not at it, major. 'Tis often the poor pressed widow's
case, to give up her honor to save her jointure, and seem to
be a light woman rather than marry, as some young men,
they say, pretend to have the filthy disease and lose their
credit with most women to avoid the importunities of some. 375

FREEMAN.

But one word with you, madam.

WIDOW.

No, no, sir. Come, major, let us make haste now to the
prerogative court.

OLDFOX.

But, lady, if what you say be true, will you stigmatize your
reputation on record? And, if it be not true, how will you 380
prove it?

WIDOW.

Pshaw! I can prove anything, and for my reputation, know,
major, a wise woman will no more value her reputation in
disinheriting a rebellious son of a good estate than she would
in getting him to inherit an estate.   385

Exeunt Widow *and* Oldfox.

FREEMAN.

Madam— We must not let her go so, squire.

JERRY.

Nay, the devil can't stop her though if she has a mind to't.
But come, bully guardian, we'll go and advise with three
attorneys, two proctors, two solicitors, and a shrewd man of
Whitefriars, neither attorney, proctor, or solicitor but as 390
pure a pimp to the law as any of them, and sure all they will
be hard enough for her, for I fear, bully guardian, you are
too good a joker to have any law in your head.

372. seem] *Q 1–2, O*; seems *Q 3–8.*

_____

390. *Whitefriars*] East End district notorious as a hangout for criminals.

FREEMAN.

    Thou'rt in the right on't, squire. I understand no law,
especially that against bastards, since I'm sure the custom is 395
against that law, and more people get estates by being so
than lose them.   *Exeunt.*

[IV.ii]   *Olivia's lodging.*
    Enter Lord Plausible *and* Boy *with a candle.*

LORD PLAUSIBLE.

    Little gentleman, your most obedient, faithful, humble ser-
vant. Where, I beseech you, is that divine person, your
noble lady?

BOY.

    Gone out, my lord, but commanded me to give you this
letter.   *Gives him a letter.* 5

            Enter to him Novel.

LORD PLAUSIBLE (*aside*).

    Which he must not observe.   *Puts it up.*

NOVEL.

    Hey, boy, where is thy lady?

BOY.

    Gone out, sir, but I must beg a word with you.

            Gives him a letter and exit.

NOVEL.

    For me? So.   *Puts up the letter.*
Servant, servant, my lord. You see the lady knew of your 10
coming, for she is gone out.

LORD PLAUSIBLE.

    Sir, I humbly beseech you not to censure the lady's good
breeding. She has reason to use more liberty with me than
with any other man.

NOVEL.

    How, viscount, how?   15

LORD PLAUSIBLE.

    Nay, I humbly beseech you, be not in choler. Where there
is most love there may be most freedom.

6. S.D. *Puts it up*] *Q5–8, O; set as
part of speech Q1–4.*

NOVEL.

Nay, then 'tis time to come to an *éclaircissement* with you and
to tell you you must think no more of this lady's love.

LORD PLAUSIBLE.

Why, under correction, dear sir?   20

NOVEL.

There are reasons, reasons, viscount.

LORD PLAUSIBLE.

What, I beseech you, noble sir?

NOVEL.

Prithee, prithee be not impertinent, my lord. Some of you
lords are such conceited, well-assured, impertinent rogues.

LORD PLAUSIBLE.

And you noble wits are so full of shamming and drolling one   25
knows not where to have you, seriously.

NOVEL.

Well, you shall find me in bed with this lady one of these
days.

LORD PLAUSIBLE.

Nay, I beseech you, spare the lady's honor, for hers and
mine will be all one shortly.   30

NOVEL.

Prithee, my lord, be not an ass. Dost thou think to get her
from me? I have had such encouragements—

LORD PLAUSIBLE.

I have not been thought unworthy of them.

NOVEL.

What, not like mine! Come to an *éclaircissement*, as I said.

LORD PLAUSIBLE.

Why, seriously then, she has told me viscountess sounded   35
prettily.

NOVEL.

And me that Novel was a name she would sooner change
hers for than for any title in England.

LORD PLAUSIBLE.

She has commended the softness and respectfulness of my
behavior.   40

NOVEL.

She has praised the briskness of my raillery of all things,
man.

LORD PLAUSIBLE.

The sleepiness of my eyes she liked.

NOVEL.

Sleepiness! Dullness, dullness. But the fierceness of mine she
adored.   45

LORD PLAUSIBLE.

The brightness of my hair she liked.

NOVEL.

The brightness! No, the greasiness, I warrant. But the
blackness and luster of mine she admires.

LORD PLAUSIBLE.

The gentleness of my smile.

NOVEL.

The subtilty of my leer.   50

LORD PLAUSIBLE.

The clearness of my complexion.

NOVEL.

The redness of my lips.

LORD PLAUSIBLE.

The whiteness of my teeth.

NOVEL.

My jaunty way of picking them.

LORD PLAUSIBLE.

The sweetness of my breath.   55

NOVEL.

Hah, ha!—Nay then she abused you, 'tis plain, for you
know what Manly said. The sweetness of your pulvillio she
might mean, but for your breath! Ha, ha, ha. Your breath
is such, man, that nothing but tobacco can perfume, and
your complexion nothing could mend but the smallpox.   60

LORD PLAUSIBLE.

Well, sir, you may please to be merry, but, to put you out of
all doubt, sir, she has received some jewels from me of value.

NOVEL.

And presents from me, besides what I presented her jaun-
tily, by way of hombre, of three or four hundred pound
value, which I'm sure are the earnest pence for our love   65
bargain.

LORD PLAUSIBLE.

Nay then, sir, with your favor and to make an end of all
your hopes look you there, sir, she has writ to me.—

NOVEL.

> How! How! Well, well, and so she has to me: look you
> there.—   *Deliver to each other their letters.* 70

LORD PLAUSIBLE.

> What's here!

NOVEL.

> How's this?   *Reads out.*

> MY DEAR LORD,

> You'll excuse me for breaking my word with you since
> 'twas to oblige, not to offend you, for I am only gone 75
> abroad to disappoint Novel and meet you in the drawing
> room, where I expect you with as much impatience as when
> I used to suffer Novel's visits, the most impertinent fop that
> ever affected the name of a wit, therefore not capable, I
> hope, to give you jealousy. For, for your sake alone, you 80
> saw, I renounced an old lover and will do all the world.
> Burn the letter but lay up the kindness of it in your heart,
> with your
>
>   OLIVIA
> Very fine! But pray let's see mine.   85

LORD PLAUSIBLE.

> I understand it not, but sure she cannot think so of me.
>
>   *Reads the other letter.*

NOVEL.

> Humh! Ha!—meet—for your sake—umh—quitted an old
> lover—world—burn—in your heart, with your
>
>   OLIVIA
> Just the same, the names only altered.   90

LORD PLAUSIBLE.

> Surely there must be some mistake, or somebody has abused
> her, and us.

NOVEL.

> Yes, you are abused, no doubt on't, my lord, but I'll to
> Whitehall and see.

LORD PLAUSIBLE.

> And I, where I shall find you are abused.   95

NOVEL.

> Where, if it be so, for our comfort we cannot fail of meeting
> with fellow-sufferers enough, for, as Freeman said of
> another, she stands in the drawing room like the glass,

ready for all comers to set their gallantry by her, and, like
the glass too, lets no man go from her unsatisfied with 100
himself.   *Exeunt ambo.*

Enter Olivia *and* Boy.

OLIVIA.
Both here and just gone?
BOY.
Yes, madam.
OLIVIA.
But are you sure neither saw you deliver the other a letter?
BOY.
Yes, yes, madam, I am very sure.   105
OLIVIA.
Go then to the Old Exchange, to Westminster, Holborn,
and all the other places I told you of, I shall not need you
these two hours. Be gone and take the candle with you and
be sure you leave word again below, I am gone out to all
that ask.   110
BOY.
Yes, madam.   *Exit.*
OLIVIA.
And my new lover will not ask I'm sure. He has his lesson
and cannot miss me here, though in the dark, which I have
purposely designed as a remedy against my blushing gallant's modesty, for young lovers like gamecocks are made 115
bolder by being kept without light.

Enter her husband Vernish *as from a journey.*

VERNISH.
Where is she? Darkness everywhere!
OLIVIA *(softly)*.
What, come before your time? My soul! My life! Your
haste has augmented your kindness and let me thank you
for it thus and thus— (*Embracing and kissing him.*) And 120

111.S.D. *Exit*] *Q1–4, Q8, O; om.*
Q5–7.

___

106. *Old Exchange . . . Holborn*] East, North, West London—in short,
all over the city.

though, my soul, the little time since you left me has seemed
an age to my impatience, sure it is yet but seven—

VERNISH.

How! Who's that you expected after seven?

OLIVIA [*aside*].

Ha! My husband returned! And have I been throwing away
so many kind kisses on my husband and wronged my lover　125
already?

VERNISH.

Speak, I say, who was it you expected after seven?

OLIVIA (*aside*).

What shall I say?—O— [*Aloud.*]　Why, 'tis but seven
days, is it, dearest, since you went out of town? And I
expected you not so soon.　　　　　　　　　　　　　　130

VERNISH.

No, sure, 'tis but five days since I left you.

OLIVIA.

Pardon my impatience, dearest, I thought them seven at
least.

VERNISH.

Nay then—

OLIVIA.

But, my life, you shall never stay half so long from me again,　135
you shan't, indeed, by this kiss, you shan't.

VERNISH.

No, no, but why alone in the dark?

OLIVIA.

Blame not my melancholy in your absence— But, my soul,
since you went, I have strange news to tell you. Manly is
returned.　　　　　　　　　　　　　　　　　　　　140

VERNISH.

Manly returned! Fortune forbid.

OLIVIA.

Met with the Dutch in the Channel, fought, sunk his ship
and all he carried with him. He was here with me yesterday.

VERNISH.

And did you own our marriage to him?

124.S.D.　*aside*] Q 2–8; *om.* Q 1, O.

OLIVIA.

I told him I was married, to put an end to his love and my 145
trouble, but to whom is yet a secret kept from him and all
the world. And I have used him so scurvily his great spirit
will ne'er return to reason it farther with me. I have sent
him to sea again, I warrant.

VERNISH.

'Twas bravely done. And sure he will now hate the shore 150
more than ever after so great a disappointment. Be you sure
only to keep awhile our great secret till he be gone. In the
meantime I'll lead the easy, honest fool by the nose as I used
to do, and whilst he stays rail with him at thee, and when
he's gone laugh with thee at him. But have you his cabinet 155
of jewels safe? Part not with a seed pearl to him to keep him
from starving.

OLIVIA.

Nor from hanging.

VERNISH.

He cannot recover them and, I think, will scorn to beg them
again.   160

OLIVIA.

But, my life, have you taken the thousand guineas he left in
my name out of the goldsmith's hands?

VERNISH.

Ay, ay, they are removed to another goldsmith's.

OLIVIA.

Ay but, my soul, you had best have a care he find not where
the money is, for his present wants, as I'm informed, are 165
such as will make him inquisitive enough.

VERNISH.

You say true and he knows the man too, but I'll remove it
tomorrow.

OLIVIA.

Tomorrow! O do not stay till tomorrow. Go tonight,
immediately.   170

VERNISH.

Now I think on't, you advise well and I will go presently.

164. he] Q1–7; you Q8, O.

OLIVIA.

Presently! Instantly! I will not let you stay a jot.

VERNISH.

I will then, though I return not home till twelve.

OLIVIA.

Nay, though not till morning with all my heart. Go dearest,
I am impatient till you are gone—   *Thrusts him out.* 175
So, I have at once now brought about those two grateful
businesses which all prudent women do together, secured
money and pleasure, and now all interruptions of the last
are removed. Go husband and come up friend, just the
buckets in the well. The absence of one brings the other, but 180
I hope like them too they will not meet in the way, justle,
and clash together.

Enter Fidelia, *and* Manly *treading softly and staying behind at some
distance.*

So, are you come? But not the husband-bucket, I hope,
again. Who's there? My dearest?   *Softly.*

FIDELIA.

My life—   185

OLIVIA.

Right, right. Where are thy lips? Here, take the dumb and
best welcomes, kisses and embraces. 'Tis not a time for idle
words. In a duel of love, as in others, parleying shows basely.
Come, we are alone, and now the word is only satisfaction
and defend not thyself.   190

MANLY (*aside*).

How's this? Wuh, she makes love like a devil in a play; and
in this darkness, which conceals her angel's face, if I were
apt to be afraid I should think her a devil.

OLIVIA.

What, you traverse ground, young gentleman.

        Fidelia *avoiding her.*

FIDELIA.

I take breath only.   195

MANLY (*aside*).

Good heavens! How was I deceived!

191. Wuh] *Q 1–5*; How   *Q 6–7*;
Why *Q 8, O.*

OLIVIA.

Nay, you are a coward. What, are you afraid of the fierceness of my love?

FIDELIA.

Yes, madam, lest its violence might presage its change and I must needs be afraid you would leave me quickly who 200 could desert so brave a gentleman as Manly.

OLIVIA.

O! Name not his name, for in a time of stolen joys, as this is, the filthy name of husband were not a more allaying sound.

MANLY (*aside*).   205

There's some comfort yet.

FIDELIA.

But did you not love him?

OLIVIA.

Never. How could you think it?

FIDELIA.

Because he thought it, who is a man of that sense, nice discerning, and diffidency that I should think it hard to deceive him.   210

OLIVIA.

No, he that distrusts most the world trusts most to himself and is but the more easily deceived because he thinks he can't be deceived. His cunning is like the coward's sword by which he is oftener worsted than defended.

FIDELIA.

Yet, sure, you used no common art to deceive him.   215

OLIVIA.

I knew he loved his own singular moroseness so well as to dote upon any copy of it, wherefore I feigned an hatred to the world too that he might love me in earnest, but if it had been hard to deceive him I'm sure 'twere much harder to love him. A dogged, ill-mannered—   220

FIDELIA (*aside to* Manly).

D'ye hear her, sir? Pray hear her.

214. than] *Q1–3, Q6–8, O*; and   221. D'ye hear her] *Q1–3, O*;
Q4–5.   D'ye hear me *Q4–8.*

OLIVIA.

Surly, untractable, snarling brute! He! A masty dog were as fit a thing to make a gallant of.

MANLY (*aside*).

Ay, a goat or monkey were fitter for thee.

FIDELIA.

I must confess for my part, though my rival, I cannot but 225 say he has a manly handsomeness in his face and mien.

OLIVIA.

So has a Saracen in the sign.

FIDELIA.

Is proper and well made.

OLIVIA.

As a drayman.

FIDELIA.

Has wit.   230

OLIVIA.

He rails at all mankind.

FIDELIA.

And undoubted courage.

OLIVIA.

Like the hangman's, can murder a man when his hands are tied. He has cruelty indeed, which is no more courage than his railing is wit.   235

MANLY (*aside*).

Thus women, and men like women, are too hard for us when they think we do not hear them, and reputation like other mistresses is never true to a man in his absence.

FIDELIA.

He is—

OLIVIA.

Prithee no more of him. I thought I had satisfied you 240 enough before that he could never be a rival for you to apprehend, and you need not be more assured of my aversion to him but by the last testimony of my love to you which I am ready to give you. Come, my soul, this way—

Pulls Fidelia.

FIDELIA.

But, madam, what could make you dissemble love to him 245

when 'twas so hard a thing for you, and flatter his love to
you?

OLIVIA.

That which makes all the world flatter and dissemble.
'Twas his money. I had a real passion for that. Yet I loved
not that so well as for it to take him, for as soon as I had 250
his money I hastened his departure like a wife who, when
she has made the most of a dying husband's breath, pulls
away the pillow.

MANLY [aside].

Damned money! Its master's potent rival still and like a
saucy pimp corrupts itself the mistress it procures for us. 255

OLIVIA.

But I did not think with you, my life, to pass my time in
talking. Come hither, come. Yet stay till I have locked a
door in the other room that might chance to let us in some
interruption, which reciting poets or losing gamesters fear
not more than I at this time do.   *Exit* Olivia. 260

FIDELIA.

Well, I hope you are now satisfied, sir, and will be gone to
think of your revenge.

MANLY.

No, I am not satisfied and must stay to be revenged.

FIDELIA.

How, sir? You'll use no violence to her, I hope, and forfeit
your own life to take away hers? That were no revenge.   265

MANLY.

No, no, you need not fear. My revenge shall only be upon
her honor, not her life.

FIDELIA.

How, sir? Her honor? O heavens! Consider, sir, she has no
honor. D'ye call that revenge? Can you think of such a
thing? But reflect, sir, how she hates and loathes you.   270

MANLY.

Yes, so much she hates me that it would be a revenge sufficient to make her accessory to my pleasure and then let
her know it.

251. his] *Q1–2, O; om. Q3–8.*   *Q8, O.*
254.S.D. *aside*] *Q6–7; om. Q1–5,*   258. might] *Q1; may Q2–8, O.*

FIDELIA.

No, sir, no, to be revenged on her now were to disappoint
her. Pray, sir, let us be gone.   *Pulls* Manly. 275

MANLY.

Hold off. What, you are my rival then and therefore you
shall stay and keep the door for me whilst I go in for you,
but when I'm gone if you dare to stir off from this very board
or breathe the least murmuring accent, I'll cut her throat
first, and if you love her you will not venture her life. Nay, 280
then I'll cut your throat too and I know you love your own
life at least.

FIDELIA.

But, sir, good sir.

MANLY.

Not a word more, lest I begin my revenge on her by killing
you.   285

FIDELIA.

But are you sure 'tis revenge that makes you do this? How
can it be?

MANLY.

Whist.

FIDELIA.

'Tis a strange revenge indeed.

MANLY.

If you make me stay, I shall keep my word and begin with 290
you. No more.

        Exit Manly *at the same door* Olivia *went. Manet* Fidelia.

FIDELIA.

O heavens! Is there not punishment enough
In loving well, if you will have it a crime,
But you must add fresh torments daily to it,
And punish us like peevish rivals still,   295
Because we fain would find a heaven here?
But did there never any love like me,
That, untried tortures, you must find me out?
Others, at worst, you force to kill themselves,
But I must be self-murderess of my love,   300

292. there not] *Q 1–7, O*; not there
Q 8.

Yet will not grant me power to end my life,
My cruel life; for when a lover's hopes
Are dead, and gone, life is unmerciful.

Sits down and weeps.

Enter Manly *to her.*

MANLY.

I have thought better on't. I must not discover myself now.
I am without witnesses, for if I barely should publish it, she 305
would deny it with as much impudence as she would act it
again with this young fellow here. Where are you?

FIDELIA.

Here—O—now I suppose we may be gone.

MANLY.

I will, but not you. You must stay and act the second part
of a lover; that is, talk kindness to her.   310

FIDELIA.

Not I, sir.

MANLY.

No disputing, sir, you must. 'Tis necessary to my design of
coming again tomorrow night.

FIDELIA.

What, can you come again then hither?

MANLY.

Yes, and you must make the appointment and an apology 315
for your leaving her so soon, for I have said not a word to
her but have kept your counsel, as I expect you should do
mine. Do this faithfully and I promise you here you shall
run my fortune still and we will never part as long as we
live, but if you do not do it expect not to live.   320

FIDELIA.

'Tis hard, sir, but such a consideration will make it easier.
You won't forget your promise, sir?

MANLY.

No, by heavens. But I hear her coming.   *Exit.*

Enter Olivia *to* Fidelia.

OLIVIA.

Where is my life? Run from me already! You do not love

305. should] *Q 1–2, O;* would *Q 3–8.*

me, dearest. Nay, you are angry with me, for you would not 325
so much as speak a kind word to me within. What was the
reason?

FIDELIA.

I was transported too much.

OLIVIA.

That's kind, but come, my soul, what make you here? Let
us go in again. We may be surprised in this room, 'tis so near 330
the stairs.

FIDELIA.

No, we shall hear the better here if anybody should come
up.

OLIVIA.

Nay, I assure you, we shall be secure enough within. Come,
come—   335

FIDELIA.

I am sick and troubled with a sudden dizziness, and cannot
stir yet.

OLIVIA.

Come, I have spirits within.

FIDELIA.

O!—don't you hear a noise, madam?

OLIVIA.

No, no, there is none. Come, come.   *Pulls her.* 340

FIDELIA.

Indeed there is, and I love you so much I must have a care
of your honor, if you won't, and go, but to come to you
tomorrow night if you please.

OLIVIA.

With all my soul, but you must not go yet. Come, prithee.

FIDELIA.

Oh!—I am now sicker and am afraid of one of my fits.   345

OLIVIA.

What fits?

FIDELIA.

Of the falling sickness, and I lie generally an hour in a
trance. Therefore pray consider your honor for the sake of
my love and let me go that I may return to you often.

OLIVIA.

But will you be sure then to come tomorrow night?   350

FIDELIA.

Yes.

OLIVIA.

Swear.

FIDELIA.

By our past kindness.

OLIVIA.

Well, go your ways then, if you will, you naughty creature
you.   *Exit* Fidelia. 355
These young lovers with their fears and modesty make
themselves as bad as old ones to us, and I apprehend their
bashfulness more than their tattling.

Fidelia *returns.*

FIDELIA.

O, madam, we're undone! There was a gentleman upon
the stairs, coming up, with a candle, which made me retire. 360
Look you, here he comes!

Enter Vernish *and his man with a light.*

OLIVIA.

How! My husband! O, undone indeed! This way.   *Exit.*

VERNISH.

Ha! You shall not escape me so, sir.   *Stops* Fidelia.

FIDELIA *(aside).*

O heavens! More fears, plagues and torments yet in store!

VERNISH.

Come, sir, I guess what your business was here, but this 365
must be your business now. Draw.   *Draws.*

FIDELIA.

Sir—

VERNISH.

No expostulations. I shall not care to hear of it. Draw.

FIDELIA.

Good sir—

VERNISH.

How, you rascal! Not courage to draw yet durst do me the 370
greatest injury in the world? Thy cowardice shall not save
thy life.   *Offers to run at* Fidelia.

FIDELIA.

O hold, sir, and send but your servant down and I'll satisfy
you, sir, I could not injure you as you imagine.

VERNISH.

Leave the light and be gone.   *Exit* Servant. 375
Now quickly, sir, what you've to say, or—

FIDELIA.

I am a woman, sir, a very unfortunate woman.

VERNISH.

How! A very handsome woman I'm sure then. Here are
witnesses of it too, I confess—

> *Pulls off her peruke and feels her breasts.*

(*Aside.*)   Well, I'm glad to find the tables turned, my wife 380
in more danger of cuckolding than I was.

FIDELIA.

Now, sir, I hope you are so much a man of honor as to let
me go now I have satisfied you, sir.

VERNISH.

When you have satisfied me, madam, I will.

FIDELIA.

I hope, sir, you are too much a gentleman to urge those 385
secrets from a woman which concern her honor. You may
guess my misfortune to be love by my disguise, but a pair
of breeches could not wrong you, sir.

VERNISH.

I may believe love has changed your outside, which could
not wrong me, but why did my wife run away?   390

FIDELIA.

I know not, sir. Perhaps because she would not be forced to
discover me to you or to guide me from your suspicions that
you might not discover me yourself, which ungentleman-
like curiosity I hope you will cease to have and let me go.

VERNISH.

Well, madam, if I must not know who you are 'twill suf- 395
fice for me only to know certainly what you are, which you
must not deny me. Come, there is a bed within, the proper
rack for lovers, and if you are a woman, there you can keep
no secrets. You'll tell me there all unasked. Come.

> *Pulls her.*

398. rack] *Q1, O*; racks *Q2–8.*

FIDELIA.

O! What d'ye mean? Help, O—   400

VERNISH.

I'll show you, but 'tis in vain to cry out. No one dares help
you, for I am lord here.

FIDELIA.

Tyrant here, but if you are master of this house, which I
have taken for sanctuary, do not violate it yourself.

VERNISH.

No, I'll preserve you here and nothing shall hurt you and 405
will be as true to you as your disguise, but you must trust
me then. Come, come.

FIDELIA.

O! O! Rather than you shall drag me to a death so horrid
and so shameful I'll die here a thousand deaths, but you do
not look like a ravisher, sir.   410

VERNISH.

Nor you like one would put me to it, but if you will—

FIDELIA.

O! O! Help, help—

Enter Servant.

VERNISH.

You saucy rascal, how durst you come in when you heard a
woman squeak? That should have been your cue to shut
the door.   415

SERVANT.

I come, sir, to let you know the alderman, coming home
immediately after you were at his house, has sent his cashier
with the money, according to your note.

VERNISH.

Damn his money! Money never came to any sure un-
seasonably till now. Bid him stay.   420

SERVANT.

He says he cannot a moment.

VERNISH.

Receive it you then.

SERVANT.

He says he must have your receipt for it. He is in haste, for I
hear him coming up, sir.

VERNISH.

Damn him. Help me in here then with this dishonorer of my 425
family.

FIDELIA.

O! O!

SERVANT.

You say she is a woman, sir.

VERNISH.

No matter, sir. Must you prate?

FIDELIA.

O heavens! Is there— 430

They thrust her in and lock the door.

VERNISH.

Stay there, my prisoner. You have a short reprieve.
I'll fetch the gold and that she can't resist;
For with a full hand 'tis we ravish best. *Exit.*

Finis actus quarti

433.1. *quarti*]　*Q 1–3,　O;　quartus*
Q 4–8.

ACT V

[V.i] *Eliza's lodging.*
Enter Olivia *and* Eliza.

OLIVIA.

Ah, cousin, nothing troubles me but that I have given the malicious world its revenge and reason now to talk as freely of me as I used to do of it.

ELIZA.

Faith, then, let not that trouble you, for to be plain, cousin, the world cannot talk worse of you than it did before.   5

OLIVIA.

How, cousin? I'd have you to know, before this faux pas, this trip of mine, the world could not talk of me.

ELIZA.

Only that you mind other people's actions so much that you take no care of your own but to hide them, that, like a thief, because you know yourself most guilty you impeach   10 your fellow criminals first to clear yourself.

OLIVIA.

O wicked world!

ELIZA.

That you pretend an aversion to all mankind in public only that their wives and mistresses may not be jealous and hinder you of their conversation in private.   15

OLIVIA.

Base world!

ELIZA.

That abroad you fasten quarrels upon innocent men for talking of you, only to bring them to ask you pardon at home and to become dear friends with them who were hardly your acquaintance before.   20

OLIVIA.

Abominable world!

ELIZA.

That you condemn the obscenity of modern plays only that you may not be censured for never missing the most obscene of the old ones.

23. not] *Q1–2, Q6–8, O; om. Q3–5.*

OLIVIA.

Damned world!   25

ELIZA.

That you deface the nudities of pictures and little statues only because they are not real.

OLIVIA.

O fie, fie, fie. Hideous, hideous, cousin! The obscenity of their censures makes me blush.

ELIZA.

The truth of them, the naughty world would say now.   30

Enter Lettice *hastily.*

LETTICE.

O! Madam, here is that gentleman coming up who now you say is my master.

OLIVIA.

O! Cousin, whither shall I run? Protect me, or—

     Olivia *runs away and stands at a distance.*

Enter Vernish.

VERNISH.

Nay, nay, come—

OLIVIA.

O, sir, forgive me.   35

VERNISH.

Yes, yes, I can forgive you being alone in the dark with a woman in man's clothes, but have a care of a man in woman's clothes.

OLIVIA *(aside).*

What does he mean? He dissembles only to get me into his power. Or has my dear friend made him believe he was a   40 woman? My husband may be deceived by him but I'm sure I was not.

VERNISH.

Come, come, you need not have lain out of your house for this, but perhaps you were afraid when I was warm with suspicions. You must have discovered who she was, and   45 prithee, may I not know it?

38. woman's] *Q 1–2*; women's *Q 3–8, O.*

OLIVIA.

She was— (*Aside.*)   I hope he has been deceived, and since
my lover has played the card I must not renounce.

VERNISH.

Come, what's the matter with thee? If I must not know
who she is, I'm satisfied without. Come hither.   50

OLIVIA.

Sure you do know her. She has told you herself, I suppose.

VERNISH.

No, I might have known her better but that I was interrupted by the goldsmith you know and was forced to lock
her into your chamber to keep her from his sight, but when
I returned I found she was got away by tying the window   55
curtains to the balcony, by which she slid down into the
street, for, you must know, I jested with her and made her
believe I'd ravish her, which she apprehended, it seems, in
earnest.

OLIVIA.

Then she got from you?   60

VERNISH.

Yes.

OLIVIA.

And is quite gone?

VERNISH.

Yes.

OLIVIA.

I'm glad on't—otherwise you had ravished her, sir? But
how dar'st you go so far as to make her believe you would   65
ravish her? Let me understand that, sir. What! There's
guilt in your face. You blush too. Nay, then you did ravish
her, you did, you base fellow. What, ravish a woman in the
first month of our marriage! 'Tis a double injury to me,
thou base ungrateful man. Wrong my bed already, villain!   70
I could tear out those false eyes, barbarous, unworthy
wretch.

ELIZA.

So, so!—

69. our] *Q 1–2, O*; her *Q 3–8.*

_____

VERNISH.

Prithee hear, my dear.

OLIVIA.

I will never hear you, my plague, my torment.   75

VERNISH.

I swear—prithee hear me.

OLIVIA.

I have heard already too many of your false oaths and
vows, especially your last in the church. O wicked man!
And wretched woman that I was! I wish I had then sunk
down into a grave rather than to have given you my hand   80
to be led to your loathsome bed. O, O—

Seems to weep.

VERNISH.

So, very fine! Just a marriage quarrel! Which, though it
generally begins by the wife's fault, yet in the conclusion
it becomes the husband's, and whosoever offends at first, he
only is sure to ask pardon at last. My dear—   85

OLIVIA.

My devil—

VERNISH.

Come, prithee be appeased and go home. I have bespoken
our supper betimes, for I could not eat till I found you. Go,
I'll give you all kind of satisfactions, and one which uses to
be a reconciling one, two hundred of those guineas I received   90
last night to do what you will with.

OLIVIA.

What, would you pay me for being your bawd?

VERNISH.

Nay, prithee no more. Go, and I'll thoroughly satisfy you
when I come home, and then too we will have a fit of
laughter at Manly, whom I am going to find at the Cock in   95
Bow Street, where, I hear, he dined. Go dearest, go home.

ELIZA *(aside).*

A very pretty turn indeed, this!

VERNISH.

Now, cousin, since by my wife I have that honor, and

93. thoroughly] *Q1;* throughly
Q2–8, O.

privilege of calling you so, I have something to beg of you
too, which is not to take notice of our marriage, to any 100
whatever, yet awhile for some reasons very important to me;
and next, that you will do my wife the honor to go home
with her and me the favor to use that power you have with
her in our reconcilement.

ELIZA.

That, I dare promise, sir, will be no hard matter. Your 105
servant.   *Exit* Vernish.
Well, cousin, this I confess was reasonable hypocrisy. You
were the better for it.

OLIVIA.

What hypocrisy?

ELIZA.

Why, this last deceit of your husband was lawful since in 110
your own defence.

OLIVIA.

What deceit? I'd have you to know I never deceived my
husband.

ELIZA.

You do not understand me, sure. I say, this was an honest
come-off and a good one, but 'twas a sign your gallant had 115
had enough of your conversation since he could so dextrously cheat your husband in passing for a woman?

OLIVIA.

What d'ye mean, once more, with my gallant and passing
for a woman?

ELIZA.

What do you mean? You see your husband took him for a 120
woman.

OLIVIA.

Whom?

ELIZA.

Heyday! Why, the man he found you with, for whom last
night you were so much afraid, and who you told me—

OLIVIA.

Lord, you rave sure!   125

ELIZA.

Why, did not you tell me last night—

OLIVIA.

I know not what I might tell you last night, in a fright.

ELIZA.

Ay, what was that fright for? For a woman? Besides, were
you not afraid to see your husband just now? I warrant,
only for having been found with a woman! Nay, did you not 130
just now too own your false step, or trip, as you called it,
which was with a woman too? Fie, this fooling is so insipid,
'tis offensive.

OLIVIA.

And fooling with my honor will be more offensive. Did you
not hear my husband say he found me with a woman in 135
man's clothes? And d'ye think he does not know a man from
a woman?

ELIZA.

Not so well, I'm sure, as you do; therefore I'd rather take
your word.

OLIVIA.

What, you grow scurrilous and are, I find, more censorious 140
than the world! I must have a care of you, I see.

ELIZA.

No, you need not fear yet. I'll keep your secret.

OLIVIA.

My secret! I'd have you to know I have no need of con-
fidants, though you value yourself upon being a good one.

ELIZA.

O admirable confidence! You show more in denying your 145
wickedness than other people in glorying in it.

OLIVIA.

Confidence, to me! To me such language! Nay, then I'll
never see your face again.   (Aside.)   I'll quarrel with her
that people may never believe I was in her power but take
for malice all the truth she may speak against me. —Lettice, 150
where are you? Let us be gone from this censorious, ill
woman.

ELIZA.

Nay, thou shalt stay a little to damn thyself quite.   (Aside.)
One word first, pray madam. Can you swear that whom
your husband found you with—   155

OLIVIA.

Swear! Ay, that whosoever 'twas that stole up, unknown, into my room when 'twas dark, I know not whether man or woman, by heavens, by all that's good, or may I never more have joys here or in the other world. Nay, may I eternally—

ELIZA.

Be damned. So, so, you are damned enough already by 160 your oaths, and I enough confirmed, and now you may please to be gone. Yet take this advice with you, in this plain-dealing age, to leave off forswearing yourself, for when people hardly think the better of a woman for her real modesty, why should you put that great constraint upon 165 yourself to feign it?

OLIVIA.

O hideous! Hideous advice! Let us go out of the hearing of it. She will spoil us, Lettice.

> *Exeunt* Olivia *and* Lettice *at one door,* Eliza *at t'other.*

[V.ii]   *The scene changes to the Cock in Bow Street.*
> *A table and bottles.*
> Manly *and* Fidelia.

MANLY.

How! Saved her honor by making her husband believe you were a woman! 'Twas well, but hard enough to do sure.

FIDELIA.

We were interrupted before he could contradict me.

MANLY.

But can't you tell me, d'ye say, what kind of man he was?

FIDELIA.

I was so frightened, I confess, I can give no other account 5 of him but that he was pretty tall, round-faced, and one I'm sure I ne'er had seen before.

MANLY.

But she, you say, made you swear to return tonight?

FIDELIA.

But I have since sworn never to go near her again, for the

3. were] *Q1–2, O*; are *Q3–4*.

husband would murder me, or worse, if he caught me   10
again.

MANLY.

No, I'll go with you and defend you tonight and then I'll
swear too never to go near her again.

FIDELIA.

Nay, indeed sir, I will not go, to be accessory to your death
too. Besides, what should you go again, sir, for?   15

MANLY.

No disputing or advice, sir. You have reason to know I am
unalterable. Go therefore presently and write her a note
to enquire if her assignation with you holds, and if not to be
at her own house, where else? And be importunate to gain
admittance to her tonight. Let your messenger ere he de-   20
liver your letter enquire first if her husband be gone out. Go,
'tis now almost six of the clock. I expect you back here
before seven with leave to see her then. Go, do this dextrously and expect the performance of my last night's
promise, never to part with you.   25

FIDELIA.

Ay, sir, but will you be sure to remember that?

MANLY.

Did I ever break my word? Go, no more replies or doubts.

Exit Fidelia.

Enter Freeman *to* Manly.

Where hast thou been?

FREEMAN.

In the next room with my Lord Plausible and Novel.

MANLY.

Ay, we came hither because 'twas a private house, but with   30
thee indeed no house can be private, for thou hast that
pretty quality of the familiar fops of the town who in an
eating house always keep company with all people in it but
those they came with.

FREEMAN.

I went into their room but to keep them and my own fool   35
the squire out of your room, but you shall be peevish now

27. ever] *Q1–2, Q6–8, O*; never
Q3–5.

because you have no money, but why the devil won't you write to those we were speaking of? Since your modesty or your spirit will not suffer you to speak to them, to lend you money, why won't you try them at last that way?   40

MANLY.

Because I know them already and can bear want better than denials, nay, than obligations.

FREEMAN.

Deny you! They cannot. All of them have been your intimate friends.

MANLY.

No, they have been people only I have obliged particularly.   45

FREEMAN.

Very well, therefore you ought to go to them the rather sure.

MANLY.

No, no. Those you have obliged most, most certainly avoid you when you can oblige them no longer, and they take your visits like so many duns. Friends, like mistresses, are avoided for obligations past.   50

FREEMAN.

Pshaw! But most of them are your relations, men of great fortune and honor.

MANLY.

Yes, but relations have so much honor as to think poverty taints the blood and disown their wanting kindred, believing, I suppose, that as riches at first makes a gentleman, the   55 want of them degrades him. But, damn them, now I'm poor I'll anticipate their contempt, and disown them.

FREEMAN.

But you have many a female acquaintance whom you have been liberal to who may have a heart to refund to you a little if you would ask it. They are not all Olivias.   60

MANLY.

Damn thee! How couldst thou think of such a thing? I would as soon rob my footman of his wages. Besides, 'twere in vain too, for a wench is like a box in an ordinary, receives all people's money easily but there's no getting, nay

64. receives] *Q1–2, O;* receive
Q3–8.

shaking, any out again, and he that fills it is sure never to   65
keep the key.

FREEMAN.

Well, but noble captain, would you make me believe that
you who know half the town, have so many friends, and
have obliged so many can't borrow fifty or an hundred
pound?   70

MANLY.

Why, noble lieutenant, you who know all the town and call
all you know friends methinks should not wonder at it,
since you find ingratitude too; for how many lords' families
(though descended from blacksmiths or tinkers) hast thou
called great and illustrious? How many ill tables called good   75
eating? How many noisy coxcombs wits? How many pert,
cocking cowards stout? How many tawdry, affected rogues
well-dressed? How many perukes admired? And how many
ill verses applauded? And yet canst not borrow a shilling.
Dost thou expect I, who always spoke truth, should?   80

FREEMAN.

Nay, now you think you have paid me, but hark you, captain, I have heard of a thing called grinning honor but
never of starving honor.

MANLY.

Well, but it has been the fate of some brave men, and if they
won't give me a ship again I can starve anywhere with a   85
musket on my shoulder.

FREEMAN.

Give you a ship! Why, you will not solicit it?

MANLY.

If I have not solicited it by my services, I know no other
way.

FREEMAN.

Your servant, sir. Nay, then I'm satisfied. I must solicit my   90
widow the closer and run the desperate fortune of matrimony on shore.   *Exit.*

Enter, to Manly, Vernish.

65. sure] *Q1, O*; surest *Q2–8.*   *8;* coaching *Q1 (DLC, ICN copies),*
77. cocking] *Q1 (DFo, ICU copies)– O.*

–148–

MANLY.

How!—Nay, here is a friend indeed, and he that has him
in his arms can know no wants.   *Embraces* Vernish.

VERNISH.

Dear sir! And he that is in your arms is secure from all fears 95
whatever. Nay, our nation is secure by your defeat at sea,
and the Dutch that fought against you have proved enemies
to themselves only in bringing you back to us.

MANLY.

Fie, fie! This from a friend? And yet from any other 'twere
unsufferable. I thought I should never have taken anything 100
ill from you.

VERNISH.

A friend's privilege is to speak his mind though it be taken
ill.

MANLY.

But your tongue need not tell me you think too well of me.
I have found it from your heart, which spoke in actions, 105
your unalterable heart. But Olivia is false, my friend, which
I suppose is no news to you.

VERNISH (*aside*).

He's in the right on't.

MANLY.

But couldst thou not keep her true to me?

VERNISH.

Not for my heart, sir.   110

MANLY.

But could you not perceive it at all before I went? Could
she so deceive us both?

VERNISH.

I must confess, the first time I knew it was three days after
your departure when she received the money you had left
in Lombard Street in her name, and her tears did not 115
hinder her it seems from counting that. You would trust her
with all, like a true, generous lover!

MANLY.

And she, like a mean jilting—

VERNISH.

Traitorous—

MANLY.

Base—   120

VERNISH.

Damned—

MANLY.

Covetous—

VERNISH.

Mercenary whore— (*Aside.*) I can hardly hold from laughing.

MANLY.

Ay, a mercenary whore indeed, for she made me pay her 125 before I lay with her.

VERNISH.

How!—Why, have you lain with her?

MANLY.

Ay, ay.

VERNISH.

Nay, she deserves you should report it at least, though you have not.   130

MANLY.

Report it! By heaven, 'tis true.

VERNISH.

How! Sure not.

MANLY.

I do not use to lie, nor you to doubt me.

VERNISH.

When?

MANLY.

Last night about seven or eight of the clock.   135

VERNISH (*aside*).

Ha!—Now I remember, I thought she spoke as if she expected some other rather than me. A confounded whore indeed!

MANLY.

But, what, thou wonderest at it! Nay, you seem to be angry too.   140

VERNISH.

I cannot but be enraged against her for her usage of you. Damned, infamous, common jade.

MANLY.

Nay, her cuckold, who first cuckolded me in my money,

shall not laugh all himself. We will do him reason, shan't
we?   145

VERNISH.

Ay, ay.

MANLY.

But thou dost not, for so great a friend, take pleasure enough
in your friend's revenge, methinks.

VERNISH.

Yes, yes, I'm glad to know it since you have lain with her.

MANLY.

Thou canst not tell me who that rascal, her cuckold, is?   150

VERNISH.

No.

MANLY.

She would keep it from you, I suppose.

VERNISH.

Yes, yes—

MANLY.

Thou wouldst laugh if thou knewest but all the circumstances of my having her. Come, I'll tell thee.   155

VERNISH.

Damn her. I care not to hear any more of her.

MANLY.

Faith, thou shalt. You must know—

Enter Freeman *backwards, endeavoring to keep out* Novel, Lord Plausible,
Jerry *and* Oldfox, *who all press in upon him.*

FREEMAN.

I tell you he has a wench with him and would be private.

MANLY.

Damn them! A man can't open a bottle in these eating
houses but presently you have these impudent, intruding, 160
buzzing flies and insects in your glass. —Well, I'll tell thee
all anon. In the meantime, prithee go to her, but not from
me, and try if you can get her to lend me but an hundred
pound of my money to supply my present wants, for I
suppose there is no recovering any of it by law.   165

VERNISH.

Not any. Think not of it, nor by this way neither.

MANLY.

Go, try, at least.

VERNISH.

I'll go, but I can satisfy you beforehand, 'twill be to no
purpose. You'll no more find a refunding wench—

MANLY.

Than a refunding lawyer; indeed their fees alike scarce ever   170
return. However, try her, put it to her.

VERNISH.

Ay, ay, I'll try her, put it to her home, with a vengeance.

                       Exit Vernish. *Manent caeteri.*

NOVEL.

Nay, you shall be our judge, Manly. Come, major, I'll speak
it to your teeth. If people provoke me to say bitter things
to their faces, they must take what follows, though, like my   175
Lord Plausible, I'd rather do it civilly behind their backs.

MANLY.

Nay, thou art a dangerous rogue, I've heard, behind a
man's back.

LORD PLAUSIBLE.

You wrong him sure, noble captain. He would do a man
no more harm behind his back than to his face.   180

FREEMAN.

I am of my lord's mind.

MANLY.

Yes, a fool, like a coward, is the more to be feared behind a
man's back more than a witty man, for as a coward is more
bloody than a brave man a fool is more malicious than a
man of wit.   185

NOVEL.

A fool, tar—a fool! Nay, thou art a brave sea judge of wit!
A fool! Prithee, when did you ever find me want something
to say, as you do often?

MANLY.

Nay, I confess thou art always talking, roaring, or making a
noise. That I'll say for thee.   190

NOVEL.

Well, and is talking a sign of a fool?

MANLY.

Yes, always talking, especially too if it be loud and fast, is
the sign of a fool.

NOVEL.

Pshaw! Talking is like fencing. The quicker the better. Run

them down, run them down. No matter for parrying. Push 195
on still, sa, sa, sa. No matter whether you argue in form,
push in guard, or no.

MANLY.

   Or hit, or no. I think thou always talkest without thinking,
Novel.

NOVEL.

   Ay, ay, studied play's the worse, to follow the allegory, as 200
the old pedant says.

OLDFOX.

   A young fop!

MANLY.

   I ever thought the man of most wit had been like him of most
money, who has no vanity in showing it everywhere, whilst
the beggarly pusher of his fortune has all he has about him 205
still only to show.

NOVEL.

   Well, sir, and makes a very pretty show in the world, let me
tell you, nay, a better than your close hunks. A pox, give
me ready money in play. What care I for a man's reputation? What are we the better for your substantial, thrifty 210
curmudgeon in wit, sir?

OLDFOX.

   Thou art a profuse young rogue indeed.

NOVEL.

   So much for talking, which I think I have proved a mark of
wit, and so is railing, roaring, and making a noise, for
railing is satire, you know, and roaring and making a noise, 215
humor.

   Enter to them Fidelia, *taking* Manly *aside and showing him a paper.*

FIDELIA.

   The hour is betwixt seven and eight exactly. 'Tis now half
an hour after six.

MANLY.

   Well, go then to the Piazza and wait for me; as soon as it is

---

   219. *Piazza*] in Covent Garden, a short distance from the Cock in Bow
Street.

quite dark I'll be with you. I must stay here yet awhile for 220
my friend.   *Exit* Fidelia.

But is railing satire, Novel?

FREEMAN.

And roaring and making a noise humor?

NOVEL.

What, won't you confess there's humor in roaring and
making a noise?   225

FREEMAN.

No.

NOVEL.

Nor in cutting napkins and hangings?

MANLY.

No, sure.

NOVEL.

Dull fops!

OLDFOX.

O rogue, rogue, insipid rogue! Nay, gentlemen, allow him 230
those things for wit, for his parts lie only that way.

NOVEL.

Peace, old fool, I wonder not at thee, but that young fellows
should be so dull as to say there's no humor in making a noise
and breaking windows! I tell you, there's wit and humor
too in both. And a wit is as well known by his frolic as by his 235
simile.

OLDFOX.

Pure rogue! There's your modern wit for you! Wit and
humor in breaking of windows! There's mischief if you will
but no wit or humor.

NOVEL.

Prithee, prithee peace, old fool. I tell you, where there is 240
mischief there's wit. Don't we esteem the monkey a wit
amongst beasts only because he's mischievous? And let me
tell you, as good nature is a sign of a fool, being mischievous
is a sign of wit.

OLDFOX.

O rogue, rogue! Pretend to be a wit by doing mischief and 245
railing!

NOVEL.

Why, thou old fool, hast no other pretense to the name of a
wit but by railing at new plays.

OLDFOX.

Thou by railing at that facetious, noble way of wit, quib-
bling.   250

NOVEL.

Thou call'st thy dullness, gravity, and thy dozing, thinking.

OLDFOX.

You, sir, your dullness, spleen. And you talk much and say
nothing.

NOVEL.

Thou readest much and understand'st nothing, sir.

OLDFOX.

You laugh loud and break no jest.   255

NOVEL.

You rail and nobody hangs himself. And thou hast nothing
of the satire but in thy face.

OLDFOX.

And you have no jest but your face, sir.

NOVEL.

Thou art an illiterate pedant.

OLDFOX.

Thou art a fool, with a bad memory.   260

MANLY.

Come, a pox on you both. You have done like wits now; for
you wits, when you quarrel, never give over till you prove
one another fools.

NOVEL.

And you fools have never any occasion of laughing at us wits
but when we quarrel; therefore let us be friends, Oldfox.   265

MANLY.

They are such wits as thou art who make the name of wit as
scandalous as that of bully, and signify a loud-laughing,
talking, incorrigible coxcomb, as bully a roaring, hardened
coward.

FREEMAN.

And would have his noise and laughter pass for wit, as   270
t'other his huffing and blustering for courage.

Enter Vernish.

262. till you] *Q 1–3*; till ye *Q 4–8, O.*

MANLY.

Gentlemen, with your leave, here is one I would speak with
and I have nothing to say to you.

Puts them out of the room. Manent Manly, Vernish.

VERNISH.

I told you 'twas in vain to think of getting money out of her.
She says, if a shilling would do it, she would not save you 275
from starving or hanging or what you would think worse,
begging or flattering, and rails so at you one would not
think you had lain with her.

MANLY.

O friend, never trust for that matter a woman's railing, for
she is no less a dissembler in her hatred than her love. And 280
as her fondness of her husband is a sign he's a cuckold,
her railing at another man is a sign she lies with him.

VERNISH (*aside*).

He's in the right on it. I know not what to trust to.

MANLY.

But you did not take any notice of it to her, I hope?

VERNISH (*aside*).

So! Sure he is afraid I should have disproved him, by an 285
enquiry of her. All may be well yet.

MANLY.

What hast thou in thy head that makes thee seem so
unquiet?

VERNISH.

Only this base, impudent woman's falseness. I cannot put
her out of my head.   290

MANLY.

O my dear friend, be not you too sensible of my wrongs, for
then I shall feel them too, with more pain, and think them
unsufferable. Damn her, her money, and that ill-natured
whore too, fortune herself; but if thou wouldst ease a little
my present trouble prithee go borrow me somewhere else 295
some money. I can trouble thee.

VERNISH.

You trouble me indeed, most sensibly, when you command
me anything I cannot do. I have lately lost a great deal of
money at play, more than I can yet pay, so that not only

295. go] *Q1–3, O*; go to *Q4–8.*

my money but my credit too is gone and I know not where 300
to borrow; but could rob a church for you. (*Aside.*) Yet
would rather end your wants, by cutting your throat.

MANLY.

Nay, then I doubly feel my poverty since I'm incapable of
supplying thee.   *Embraces* Vernish.

VERNISH.

But methinks she that granted you the last favor, as they 305
call it, should not deny you anything.

NOVEL.

Hey, tarpaulin, have you done?

                    Novel *looks in and retires again.*

VERNISH.

I understand not that point of kindness, I confess.

MANLY.

No, thou dost not understand it and I have not time to let
you know all now, for these fools, you see, will interrupt us; 310
but anon, at supper, we'll laugh at leisure together at
Olivia's cuckold, who took a young fellow that goes
between his wife and me, for a woman.

VERNISH.

Ha!

MANLY.

Senseless, easy rascal! 'Twas no wonder she chose him for a 315
husband, but she thought him, I thank her, fitter than me
for that blind, bearing office.

VERNISH (*aside*).

I could not be deceived in that long woman's hair tied up
behind, nor those infallible proofs, her pouting, swelling
breasts. I have handled too many sure not to know them.   320

MANLY.

What, you wonder the fellow could be such a blind
coxcomb!

VERNISH.

Yes, yes—   Novel *looks in again and retires.*

NOVEL.

Nay, prithee come to us, Manly. Gad, all the fine things
one says in their company are lost without thee.   325

325. in] *Q1–8, O; one state of Q2*
omits the "i."

MANLY.

> Away, fop, I'm busy yet. You see we cannot talk here at our
> ease; besides, I must be gone immediately in order to
> meeting with Olivia again tonight.

VERNISH.

> Tonight! It cannot be sure—

MANLY.

> I had an appointment just now from her.				330

VERNISH.

> For what time?

MANLY.

> At half an hour after seven precisely.

VERNISH.

> Don't you apprehend the husband?

MANLY.

> He! Sniveling gull! He a thing to be feared! A husband, the
> tamest of creatures!						335

VERNISH (*aside*).

> Very fine!

MANLY.

> But, prithee, in the meantime go try to get me some money.
> Though thou art too modest to borrow for thyself, thou
> canst do anything for me, I know. Go, for I must be gone to
> Olivia. Go and meet me here anon. —Freeman, where are 340
> you?					*Exit* Manly. *Manet* Vernish.

VERNISH.

> Ay, I'll meet with you, I warrant, but it shall be at Olivia's.
> Sure it cannot be. She denies it so calmly and with that
> honest, modest assurance, it can't be true—and he does not
> use to lie—but belying a woman when she won't be kind is 345
> the only lie a brave man will least scruple. But then the
> woman in man's clothes, whom he calls a man! Well but by
> her breasts I know her to be a woman. But then again
> his appointment from her to meet with him tonight! I
> am distracted more with doubt than jealousy. Well, I have 350
> no way to disabuse or revenge myself but by going home
> immediately, putting on a riding suit, and pretending to my

341. S.D. *Manet*] *Q1, Q8, O; Manent
Q2; Enter Q4–7.*

wife the same business which carried me out of town last
requires me again to go post to Oxford tonight. Then, if
the appointment he boasts of be true, it's sure to hold, and I   355
shall have an opportunity either of clearing her or revenging
myself on both. Perhaps she is his wench of an old date and
I am his cully whilst I think him mine, and he has seemed
to make his wench rich only that I might take her off of his
hands. Or if he has but lately lain with her, he must needs   360
discover, by her, my treachery to him, which I'm sure he
will revenge with my death and which I must prevent with
his, if it were only but for fear of his too just reproaches. For,
I must confess, I never had till now any excuse but that of
interest for doing ill to him.   *Exit* Vernish.   365

Re-enter Manly *and* Freeman.

MANLY.

Come hither, only I say be sure you mistake not the time.
You know the house exactly where Olivia lodges. 'Tis just
hard by.

FREEMAN.

Yes, yes.

MANLY.

Well then, bring them all, I say, thither, and all you know   370
that may be then in the house, for the more witnesses I have
of her infamy the greater will be my revenge. And be sure
you come straight up to her chamber without more ado.
Here, take the watch. You see 'tis above a quarter past
seven. Be there in half an hour exactly.   375

FREEMAN.

You need not doubt my diligence or dexterity. I am an old
scourer and can naturally beat up a wench's quarters that
won't be civil. Shan't we break her windows too?

MANLY.

No, no. Be punctual only.   *Exeunt ambo.*

Enter Widow Blackacre, *and two* Knights of the Post, *and a* Waiter
with wine.

359. of] *Q1; om. Q2–8, O.*   379. S.D. *ambo] Q1–7, O; om. Q8.*
373. straight] *Q4–8, O;* strait *Q1–3.*

WIDOW.

    Sweetheart, are you sure the door was shut close that none 380
of those roisters saw us come in?

WAITER.

    Yes, mistress, and you shall have a privater room above
instantly.   *Exit* Waiter.

WIDOW.

    You are safe enough, gentlemen, for I have been private in
this house ere now upon other occasions when I was some- 385
thing younger. Come, gentlemen, in short, I leave my
business to your care and fidelity and so, here's to you.

1 KNIGHT.

    We were ungrateful rogues if we should not be honest to
you, for we have had a great deal of your money.

WIDOW.

    And you have done me many a good job for it, and so, here's 390
to you again.

2 KNIGHT.

    Why, we have been perjured but six times for you.

1 KNIGHT.

    Forged but four deeds with your husband's last deed of gift.

2 KNIGHT.

    And but three wills.

1 KNIGHT.

    And counterfeited hands and seals to some six bonds. I 395
think that's all, brother.

WIDOW.

    Ay, that's all, gentlemen, and so, here's to you again.

2 KNIGHT.

    Nay, 'twould do one's heart good to be forsworn for you.
You have a conscience in your ways and pay us well.

1 KNIGHT.

    You are in the right on't, brother; one would be damned 400
for her with all one's heart.

2 KNIGHT.

    But there are rogues who make us forsworn for them and
when we come to be paid they'll be forsworn too and not
pay us our wages which they promised with oaths sufficient.

388. were] *Q 1–2*; are *Q 3–8*, *O*.

1 KNIGHT.

Ay, a great lawyer, that shall be nameless, bilked me too. 405

WIDOW.

That was hard, methinks, that a lawyer should use gentlemen witnesses no better.

2 KNIGHT.

A lawyer! D'ye wonder a lawyer should do it? I was bilked
by a reverend divine that preaches twice on Sundays and
prays half an hour still before dinner.   410

WIDOW.

How? A conscientious divine and not pay people for damning themselves! Sure then, for all his talking he does not
believe damnation. But come, to our business. Pray be sure
to imitate exactly the flourish at the end of this name.

Pulls out a deed or two.

1 KNIGHT.

O he's the best in England at untangling a flourish, madam. 415

WIDOW.

And let not the seal be a jot bigger. Observe well the dash
too at the end of this name.

2 KNIGHT.

I warrant you, madam.

WIDOW.

Well, these and many other shifts poor widows are put to
sometimes, for everybody would be riding a widow, as they 420
say, and breaking into her jointure. They think marrying a
widow an easy business, like leaping the hedge where another
has gone over before. A widow is a mere gap, a gap with
them.

Enter to them Major Oldfox *with two waiters. The* Knights of the Post
huddle up the writings.

What, he here! Go then, go, my hearts, you have your 425
instructions.   *Exeunt* Knights of the Post.

OLDFOX.

Come, madam, to be plain with you, I'll be fobbed off no
longer. (*Aside.*)   I'll bind her and gag her but she shall
hear me. —Look you, friends, there's the money I promised
you, and now do you what you promised me. Here are my 430
garters and here's a gag. You shall be acquainted with my
parts, lady, you shall.

WIDOW.

Acquainted with your parts! A rape, a rape— What, will
you ravish me?

> *The waiters tie her to the chair and gag her, and exeunt.*

OLDFOX.

Yes, lady, I will ravish you, but it shall be through the ear,   435
lady, the ear only, with my well-penned acrostics.

Enter to them Freeman, Jerry Blackacre, *three* Bailiffs, *a constable and
his assistants, with the two* Knights of the Post.

What, shall I never read my things undisturbed again?

JERRY.

O law! My mother bound hand and foot and gaping as if
she rose before her time today!

FREEMAN.

What means this, Oldfox? But I'll release you from him.   440
You shall be no man's prisoner but mine. Bailiffs, execute
your writ.   Freeman *unties her.*

OLDFOX.

Nay, then I'll be gone for fear of being bail and paying her
debts without being her husband.   *Exit* Oldfox.

1 BAILIFF.

We arrest you, in the king's name at the suit of Mr. Free-   445
man, guardian to Jeremiah Blackacre, Esquire, in an action
of ten thousand pounds.

WIDOW.

How! How! In a choke-bail action! What, and the pen-
and-ink gentlemen taken too! Have you confessed, you
rogues?   450

1 KNIGHT.

We needed not to confess, for the bailiffs dogged us hither
to the very door and overheard all that you and we said.

WIDOW.

Undone, undone then! No man was ever too hard for me till
now. O, Jerry, child, wilt thou vex again the womb that
bore thee?   455

JERRY.

Ay, for bearing me before wedlock, as you say. But I'll

454. O,] *Q1–2, O; om. Q3–8.*

---

448. *choke-bail action*] a suit in which bail is not allowable.

teach you to call a Blackacre a bastard, though you were
never so much my mother.

WIDOW.

Well, I'm undone. Not one trick left? No law-meush
imaginable? (*Aside.*) Cruel sir, a word with you I pray. 460

FREEMAN.

In vain, madam, for you have no other way to release
yourself but by the bonds of matrimony.

WIDOW.

How, sir, how! That were but to sue out an *habeas corpus* for
a removal from one prison to another. Matrimony!

FREEMAN.

Well, bailiffs, away with her. 465

WIDOW.

O stay, sir, can you be so cruel as to bring me under covert
baron again and put it out of my power to sue in my own
name? Matrimony, to a woman, is worse than excom-
munication in depriving her of the benefit of the law,
and I would rather be deprived of life. But hark you, sir, I 470
am contented you should hold and enjoy my person by
lease or patent but not by the spiritual patent called a license;
that is, to have the privileges of a husband without the
dominion; that is, *durante beneplacito,* in consideration of
which I will, out of my jointure, secure you an annuity 475
of three hundred pounds a year and pay your debts, and
that's all you younger brothers desire to marry a widow for,
I'm sure.

FREEMAN.

Well, widow, if—

JERRY.

What, I hope, bully guardian, you are not making agree- 480
ments without me?

FREEMAN.

No, no. First, widow, you must say no more that he is the
son of a whore. Have a care of that. And then he must have
a settled exhibition of forty pounds a year and a nag of

---

459. *law-meush*] loophole.
474. *durante beneplacito*] so long as one gives satisfaction.
484. *exhibition*] a benefaction for maintenance.
484–485. *nag of assizes*] a first-class horse.

assizes, kept by you, but not upon the common, and have 485
free ingress, egress, and regress to and from your maids'
garret.

WIDOW.

Well, I can grant all that too.

JERRY.

Ay, ay, fair words butter no cabbage, but, guardian, make
her sign, sign and seal, for otherwise, if you knew her as well 490
as I, you would not trust her word for a farthing.

FREEMAN.

I warrant thee, squire. Well, widow, since thou are so
generous too, and if you will secure me four hundred
pound a year, but during your life and pay my debts, not
above a thousand pound, I'll bate you your person to dispose 495
of as you please.

WIDOW.

Have a care, sir, a settlement without a consideration is void
in law. You must do something for it.

FREEMAN.

Prithee then let the settlement on me be called alimony and
the consideration our separation. Come, my lawyer, with 500
writings ready drawn, is within and in haste. Come.

WIDOW.

But, what, no other kind of consideration, Mr. Freeman?
Well, a widow, I see, is a kind of a *sine cure*, by custom of
which the unconscionable incumbent enjoys the profits without any duty but does that still elsewhere.   *Exeunt omnes.* 505

[V.iii]   *The scene changes to Olivia's lodging.*
               Enter Olivia *with a candle in her hand.*

OLIVIA.

So, I am now prepared once more for my timorous young
lover's reception. My husband is gone and go thou out too,
thou next interrupter of love.   (*Puts out the candle.*)   Kind
darkness that frees us lovers from scandal and bashfulness,
from the censure of our gallants and the world. So, are you   5
there?

---

494. pound] *Q1–2, Q8, O*; pounds   498. in law] *Q1, O*; in the law
Q3–7.   *Q2–8.*

Enter to Olivia, Fidelia, *followed softly by* Manly.

Come, my dear punctual lover, there is not such another in
the world; thou hast beauty and youth to please a wife,
address and wit to amuse and fool a husband. Nay, thou
hast all things to be wished in a lover but your fits. I hope,   10
my dear, you won't have one tonight and, that you may not,
I'll lock the door though there be no need of it but to lock
out your fits, for my husband is just gone out of town again.
Come, where are you?   *Goes to the door and locks it.*

MANLY (*aside*).

Well, thou hast impudence enough to give me fits too and   15
make revenge itself impotent, hinder me from making thee
yet more infamous, if it can be.

OLIVIA.

Come, come, my soul, come.

FIDELIA.

Presently, my dear. We have time enough sure.

OLIVIA.

How! Time enough! True lovers can no more think they   20
ever have time enough than love enough. You shall stay
with me all night, but that is but a lover's moment. Come.

FIDELIA.

But won't you let me give you and myself the satisfaction of
telling you how I abused your husband last night?

OLIVIA.

Not when you can give me and yourself too the satisfaction   25
of abusing him again tonight. Come.

FIDELIA.

Let me but tell you how your husband—

OLIVIA.

O name not his or Manly's more loathsome name, if you
love me. I forbid them last night, and you know I mentioned my husband but once and he came. No talking,   30
pray; 'twas ominous to us. You make me fancy a noise at
the door already, but I'm resolved not to be interrupted.
(*A noise at the door.*)   Where are you? Come, for rather than
lose my dear expectation now, though my husband were at

17. yet] *Q1–3, O; om. Q4–8.*

the door and the bloody ruffian Manly here in the room with   35
all his awful insolence, I would give myself to this dear hand,
to be led away to heavens of joys which none but thou
canst give. But what's this noise at the door? So, I told you
what talking would come to.   (*The noise at the door increases.*)
Ha!—O heavens, my husband's voice!—   40
                                               Olivia listens at the door.

MANLY (*aside*).

Freeman is come too soon.

OLIVIA.

O 'tis he!—Then here is the happiest minute lost that ever
bashful boy or trifling woman fooled away! I'm undone!
My husband's reconcilement too was false, as my joy, all
delusion. But, come this way. Here's a back door.   45
                                               Exit and returns.
The officious jade has locked us in instead of locking others
out, but let us then escape your way, by the balcony, and,
whilst you pull down the curtains, I'll fetch from my closet
what next will best secure our escape. I have left my key in
the door and 'twill not suddenly be broke open.   *Exit.*   50
                          A noise as it were people forcing the door.

MANLY.

Stir not, yet fear nothing.

FIDELIA.

Nothing but your life, sir.

MANLY.

We shall now know this happy man she calls husband.

                            Olivia *re-enters.*

OLIVIA.

O, where are you? What, idle with fear? Come, I'll tie the
curtains if you will hold. Here, take this cabinet and purse,   55
for it is thine if we escape.
                    Manly *takes from her the cabinet and purse.*
Therefore let us make haste.   *Exit* Olivia.

MANLY.

'Tis mine indeed now again and it shall never escape more
from me, to you at least.

36. insolence]   *Q 1–6,*   *Q 8,*   *O;*
insolences *Q 7.*

The door broken open, enter Vernish *alone with a dark lantern and a sword running at* Manly, *who draws, puts by the thrust, and defends himself, whilst* Fidelia *runs at* Vernish *behind.*

VERNISH (*with a low voice*).

So, there I'm right sure—   60

MANLY (*softly*).

Sword and dark lantern, villain, are some odds, but—

VERNISH (*with a low voice*).

Odds! I'm sure I find more odds than I expected. What, has
my insatiable two seconds at once? But—

Whilst they fight, Olivia *re-enters, tying two curtains together.*

OLIVIA.

Where are you now?—What, is he entered then and are
they fighting? O do not kill one that can make no defense.   65
(Manly *throws* Vernish *down and disarms him.*)   How! But I
think he has the better on't. Here's his scarf, 'Tis he. So
keep him down still. I hope thou hast no hurt, my dearest?
Embraces Manly.

Enter to them Freeman, Lord Plausible, Novel, Jerry Blackacre, *and
the* Widow Blackacre, *lighted in by the two sailors with torches.*

Ha!—What?—Manly! And have I been thus concerned
for him, embracing him? And has he his jewels again too?   70
What means this? O 'tis too sure, as well as my shame,
which I'll go hide forever.   *Offers to go out.* Manly *stops her.*

MANLY.

No, my dearest, after so much kindness as has passed
between us, I cannot part with you yet. Freeman, let
nobody stir out of the room, for, notwithstanding your   75
lights, we are yet in the dark till this gentleman please to
turn his face.   *Pulls* Vernish *by the sleeve.*
How! Vernish! Art thou the happy man then? Thou! Thou!
Speak, I say. But thy guilty silence tells me all. —Well, I
shall not upbraid thee, for my wonder is striking me as   80
dumb as thy shame has made thee. But, what? My little
volunteer hurt and fainting!

59.1. *broken*] *Q 1–4; broke Q 5–8, O.*   72. S.D. *out.* Manly] *Q 1–3; out and*
68.3. *in*] *Q 1–7; om. Q 8, O.*   Manly *Q 4–8, O.*

FIDELIA.

My wound, sir, is but a slight one, in my arm. 'Tis only my
fear of your danger, sir, not yet well over.

MANLY.

But what's here? More strange things!   85

Observing Fidelia's *hair untied behind and without a peruke, which she lost
in the scuffle.*

What means this long woman's hair and face? Now all of
it appears, too beautiful for a man, which I still thought
womanish indeed! What, you have not deceived me too,
my little volunteer?

OLIVIA (*aside*).

Me she has I'm sure.   90

MANLY

Speak.

Enter Eliza *and* Lettice.

ELIZA.

What, cousin, I am brought hither by your woman, I
suppose, to be a witness of the second vindication of your
honor?

OLIVIA.

Insulting is not generous. You might spare me. I have you. 95

ELIZA.

Have a care, cousin, You'll confess anon too much, and I
would not have your secrets.

MANLY (*to* Fidelia).

Come, your blushes answer me sufficiently and you have
been my volunteer in love.

FIDELIA.

I must confess I needed no compulsion to follow you all the 100
world over, which I attempted in this habit, partly out of
shame to own my love to you and fear of a greater shame,
your refusal of it. For I knew of your engagement to this lady
and the constancy of your nature, which nothing could
have altered but herself.   105

MANLY.

Dear madam, I desired you to bring me out of confusion

103. knew] *Q1–2, Q5–8, O*; know
Q3–4.

and you have given me more. I know not what to speak to
you or how to look upon you. The sense of my rough, hard,
and ill usage of you, though chiefly your own fault, gives me
more pain now 'tis over than you had when you suffered it; 110
and if my heart, the refusal of such a woman (*pointing to*
Olivia), were not a sacrifice to profane your love and a
greater wrong to you than ever yet I did you, I would beg
of you to receive it, though you used it as she had done; for
though it deserved not from her the treatment she gave it, 115
it does from you.

FIDELIA.

Then it has had punishment sufficient from her already and
needs no more from me, and, I must confess, I would not
be the only cause of making you break your last night's oath
to me of never parting with me, if you do not forget or repent 120
it.

MANLY.

Then, take forever my heart and this with it.   (*Gives her the
cabinet.*)   For 'twas given to you before, and my heart was
before your due. I only beg leave to dispose of these few—
Here, madam, I never yet left my wench unpaid.   125

Takes some of the jewels and offers them to Olivia. *She strikes them down.*
Plausible *and* Novel *take them up.*

OLIVIA.

So it seems, by giving her the cabinet.

LORD PLAUSIBLE.

These pendants appertain to your most faithful, humble
servant.

NOVEL.

And this locket is mine, my earnest for love, which she never
paid, therefore my own again.   130

WIDOW.

By what law, sir, pray? Cousin Olivia, a word. What, do
they make a seizure on your goods and chattels, *vi et armis*?

119. night's] *Q 1–4, Q 8, O*; night
Q 5–7.

---

132. *vi et armis*] by force of arms.

Make your demand, I say, and bring your trover, bring your trover. I'll follow the law for you.

OLIVIA.

And I my revenge.   *Exit* Olivia. 135

MANLY (to Vernish).

But 'tis, my friend, in your consideration most that I would have returned part of your wife's portion, for 'twere hard to take all from thee, since thou hast paid so dear for it in being such a rascal. Yet thy wife is a fortune without a portion and thou art a man of that extraordinary merit in 140 villainy, the world and fortune can never desert thee, though I do; therefore be not melancholy. Fare you well, sir.   *Exit* Vernish *doggedly.*

Now, madam, I beg your pardon (*turning to* Fidelia), for lessening the present I made you, but my heart can never 145 be lessened. This, I confess, was too small for you before, for you deserve the Indian world, and I would now go thither out of covetousness for your sake only.

FIDELIA.

Your heart, sir, is a present of that value I can never make any return to it. (*Pulling* Manly *from the company.*) But I 150 can give you back such a present as this, which I got by the loss of my father, a gentleman of the North, of no mean extraction, whose only child I was, therefore left me in the present possession of two thousand pounds a year, which I left, with multitudes of pretenders, to follow you, sir, having 155 in several public places seen you and observed your actions thoroughly, with admiration, when you were too much in love to take notice of mine, which yet was but too visible. The name of my family is Grey, my other Fidelia. The rest of my story you shall know when I have fewer auditors.   160

MANLY.

Nay, now, madam, you have taken from me all power of making you any compliment on my part, for I was going to tell you that for your sake only I would quit the unknown pleasure of a retirement and stay in this ill world of ours still, though odious to me, than give you more frights again 165

133. bring your trover] *Q 1–6, Q 8,*
O; Q 7 omits repetition.

at sea and make again too great a venture there in you
alone. But if I should tell you now all this, and that your
virtue (since greater than I thought any was in this world)
had now reconciled me to it, my friend here would say, 'tis
your estate that has made me friends with the world.   170

FREEMAN.

I must confess I should, for I think most of our quarrels to
the world are just such as we have to a handsome woman,
only because we cannot enjoy her as we would do.

MANLY.

Nay, if thou art a plain dealer too, give me thy hand, for
now I'll say I am thy friend indeed. And, for your two 175
sakes, though I have been so lately deceived in friends of
both sexes,

    I will believe there are now in the world
    Good-natured friends who are not prostitutes,
    And handsome women worthy to be friends.   180
    Yet for my sake let no one e'er confide
    In tears or oaths, in love or friend untried.

Exeunt Omnes.

FINIS

175. two] *Q 1–2, O; om. Q 3–8.*   182. tears] *Q 1–2, Q 5–8, O;* years
                                                 Q 3–4.

EPILOGUE

Spoken by the Widow Blackacre

To you, the judges learned in stage laws,
Our poet now, by me, submits his cause;
For with young judges, such as most of you,
The men by women best their business do:
And, truth on't is, if you did not sit here,   5
To keep for us a term throughout the year,
We could not live by'r tongues; nay, but for you,
Our chamber-practice would be little too.
And 'tis not only the stage practiser
Who, by your meeting, gets her living here;   10
For, as in Hall of Westminster,
Sleek semptress vents, amidst the courts, her ware:
So, while we bawl, and you in judgment sit,
The visor-mask sells linen too in the pit.
O many of your friends, besides us here,   15
Do live, by putting off their several ware.
Here's daily done the great affair of the nation:
Let love, and us then, ne'er have long vacation.
But hold; like other pleaders, I have done
Not my poor client's business, but my own.   20
Spare me a word then, now, for him. First know,
Squires of the long robe, he does humbly show
He has a just right in abusing you;
Because he is a brother-templer too:
For, at the bar, you railly one another;   25
And fool, and knave, is swallowed from a brother:
If not the poet here, the templar spare;
And maul him, when you catch him at the bar.
From you, our common modish censurers,
Your favor, not your judgment, 'tis he fears: 30
Of all loves begs you then to rail, find fault;
For plays, like women, by the world are thought.
(When you speak kindly of 'em) very naught.

---

14. *visor-mask sells linen*] prostitute solicits customers.
22. *Squires . . . robe*] law students, also called Templers, from their
residence.

Appendix

Chronology

Approximate dates are indicated by *. Dates for plays are those on which they were first made public, either on stage or in print.

Political and Literary Events	*Life and Major Works of Wycherley*
1631 Death of Donne. John Dryden born.	
1633 Samuel Pepys born.	
1635 Sir George Etherege born.*	
1640 Aphra Behn born.*	
1641	Born* at Clive, near Shrewsbury, into a Royalist family of good estate.
1642 First Civil War began (ended 1646). Theaters closed by Parliament. Thomas Shadwell born.*	
1648 Second Civil War.	
1649 Execution of Charles I.	
1650 Jeremy Collier born.	
1651 Hobbes' *Leviathan* published.	
1652 First Dutch War began (ended 1654).	

Thomas Otway born.

1653
Nathaniel Lee born.*

1656
D'Avenant's *THE SIEGE OF RHODES* performed at Rutland House.

At fifteen,* sent to France for his education; associated with the Marquise de Montausier and her *précieux* circle.

1657
John Dennis born.

1658
Death of Oliver Cromwell.
D'Avenant's *THE CRUELTY OF THE SPANIARDS IN PERU* performed at the Cockpit.

1660
Restoration of Charles II.
Theatrical patents granted to Thomas Killigrew and Sir William D'Avenant, authorizing them to form, respectively, the King's and the Duke of York's Companies.
Pepys began his diary.

Converted to Catholicism.
Returned to England; entered Queen's College, Oxford, in July.
Reconverted to Church of England.
Entered Inner Temple in November.

1661
Cowley's *THE CUTTER OF COLEMAN STREET.*
D'Avenant's *THE SIEGE OF RHODES* (expanded to two parts).

1662
Charter granted to the Royal Society.

1663
Dryden's *THE WILD GALLANT.*
Tuke's *THE ADVENTURES OF FIVE HOURS.*

1664
Sir John Vanbrugh born.
Dryden's *THE RIVAL LADIES.*
Dryden and Howard's *THE INDIAN QUEEN.*

Etherege's *THE COMICAL RE-
VENGE.*

1665
Second Dutch War began (ended
1667).
Great Plague.
Dryden's *THE INDIAN EM-
PEROR.*
Orrery's *MUSTAPHA.*

1666
Fire of London.
Death of James Shirley.

1667
Jonathan Swift born.
Milton's *Paradise Lost* published.
Sprat's *The History of the Royal
Society* published.
Dryden's *SECRET LOVE.*

1668
Death of D'Avenant.
Dryden made Poet Laureate.
Dryden's *An Essay of Dramatic
Poesy* published.
Shadwell's *THE SULLEN
LOVERS.*

1669
Pepys terminated his diary.
Susannah Centlivre born.

1670
William Congreve born.
Dryden's *THE CONQUEST OF
GRANADA*, Part I.

1671
Dorset Garden Theatre (Duke's
Company) opened.
Colley Cibber born.
Milton's *Paradise Regained* and *Sam-
son Agonistes* published.
Dryden's *THE CONQUEST OF
GRANADA*, Part II.
THE REHEARSAL, by the Duke
of Buckingham and others.

Performance (March*) of *LOVE
IN A WOOD; OR, ST. JAMES'S
PARK*, a comedy which won him
the favor of the Duchess of Cleve-
land, and indirectly of the Duke of
Buckingham.

1672
Third Dutch War began (ended 1674).
Joseph Addison born.
Richard Steele born.
Dryden's *MARRIAGE À LA MODE.*

Performance (August*) of *THE GENTLEMAN DANCING-MASTER*, a less successful comedy.

1674
New Drury Lane Theatre (King's Company) opened.
Death of Milton.
Nicholas Rowe born.
Thomas Rymer's *Reflections on Aristotle's Treatise of Poesy* (translation of Rapin) published.

1675
Dryden's *AURENG-ZEBE.*

Performance in January of *THE COUNTRY WIFE.*

1676
Etherege's *THE MAN OF MODE.*
Otway's *DON CARLOS.*
Shadwell's *THE VIRTUOSO.*

Performance in December of *THE PLAIN DEALER*, from whose protagonist he acquired the name of "Manly" Wycherley.

1677
Rymer's *Tragedies of the Last Age Considered* published.
Aphra Behn's *THE ROVER.*
Dryden's *ALL FOR LOVE.*
Lee's *THE RIVAL QUEENS.*

1678
Popish Plot.
George Farquhar born.
Bunyan's *Pilgrim's Progress* (Part I) published.

Illness; visited France for his health, with financial aid from the King.

1679
Exclusion Bill introduced.
Death of Thomas Hobbes.
Death of Roger Boyle, Earl of Orrery.
Charles Johnson born.

1680
Death of Samuel Butler.

Secret marriage to the widowed

Death of John Wilmot, Earl of Rochester.
Dryden's THE SPANISH FRIAR.
Lee's LUCIUS JUNIUS BRUTUS.
Otway's THE ORPHAN.

Countess of Drogheda incurred the displeasure of the King, who had offered Wycherley the tutorship of his son, the young Duke of Richmond.

1681
Charles II dissolved Parliament at Oxford.
Dryden's Absalom and Achitophel published.
Tate's adaptation of KING LEAR.

Death of wife; involved in lawsuits with her family.

1682
The King's and the Duke of York's Companies merged into the United Company.
Dryden's The Medal, MacFlecknoe, and Religio Laici published.
Otway's VENICE PRESERVED.

Put into Fleet Prison for debt.

1683
Rye House Plot.
Death of Thomas Killigrew.
Crowne's CITY POLITIQUES.

1685
Death of Charles II; accession of James II.
Revocation of the Edict of Nantes.
The Duke of Monmouth's Rebellion.
Death of Otway.
John Gay born.
Crowne's SIR COURTLY NICE.
Dryden's ALBION AND ALBANIUS.

1686

Freed by James II; given pension of £200.

1687
Death of the Duke of Buckingham.
Dryden's The Hind and the Panther published.
Newton's Principia published.

Reconverted to Catholicism.

1688

The Revolution.

Alexander Pope born.

Shadwell's *THE SQUIRE OF ALSATIA.*

1689

The War of the League of Augsburg began (ended 1697).

Toleration Act.

Death of Aphra Behn.

Shadwell made Poet Laureate.

Dryden's *DON SEBASTIAN.*

Shadwell's *BURY FAIR.*

Lost pension after the Revolution. In debt, retired to Clive; a Jacobite.

1690

Battle of the Boyne.

Locke's *Two Treatises of Government* and *An Essay Concerning Human Understanding* published.

1691

Death of Etherege.*

Langbaine's *An Account of the English Dramatic Poets* published.

1692

Death of Lee.

Death of Shadwell.

Tate made Poet Laureate.

1693

George Lillo born.*

Rymer's *A Short View of Tragedy* published.

Congreve's *THE OLD BACHELOR.*

1694

Death of Queen Mary.

Southerne's *THE FATAL MAR-RIAGE.*

1695

Group of actors led by Thomas Betterton left Drury Lane and established a new company at Lincoln's Inn Fields.

Congreve's *LOVE FOR LOVE.*

Southerne's *OROONOKO.*

1696
Cibber's *LOVE'S LAST SHIFT.*
Vanbrugh's *THE RELAPSE.*

1697
Treaty of Ryswick ended the War
of the League of Augsburg.
Charles Macklin born.
Congreve's *THE MOURNING
BRIDE.*
Vanbrugh's *THE PROVOKED
WIFE.*

Death of litigious father Daniel.
Returned to London.

1698
Collier controversy started with the
publication of *A Short View of the
Immorality and Profaneness of the
English Stage.*

1699
Farquhar's *THE CONSTANT
COUPLE.*

1700
Death of Dryden.
Blackmore's *Satire against Wit* pub-
lished.
Congreve's *THE WAY OF THE
WORLD.*

1701
Act of Settlement.
War of the Spanish Succession
began (ended 1713).
Death of James II.
Rowe's *TAMERLANE.*
Steele's *THE FUNERAL.*

1702
Death of William III; accession of
Anne.
The Daily Courant began publication.
Cibber's *SHE WOULD AND SHE
WOULD NOT.*

1703
Death of Samuel Pepys.
Rowe's *THE FAIR PENITENT.*

1704

Capture of Gibraltar; Battle of Blenheim.

Defoe's *The Review* began publication (1704–1713).

Swift's *A Tale of a Tub* and *The Battle of the Books* published.

Cibber's *THE CARELESS HUSBAND*.

Publication of *Miscellany Poems* led to friendship with the young Alexander Pope.

1705

Haymarket Theatre opened.

Steele's *THE TENDER HUSBAND*.

1706

Battle of Ramillies.

Farquhar's *THE RECRUITING OFFICER*.

1707

Union of Scotland and England.

Death of Farquhar.

Henry Fielding born.

Farquhar's *THE BEAUX' STRATAGEM*.

1708

Downes' *Roscius Anglicanus* published.

1709

Samuel Johnson born.

Rowe's edition of Shakespeare published.

The Tatler began publication (1709–1711).

Centlivre's *THE BUSY BODY*.

1711

Shaftesbury's *Characteristics* published.

The Spectator began publication (1711–1712).

Pope's *An Essay on Criticism* published.

1713

Treaty of Utrecht ended the War of the Spanish Succession.

Addison's *CATO*.

1714
Death of Anne; accession of
George I.
Steele became Governor of Drury
Lane.
John Rich assumed management of
Lincoln's Inn Fields.
Centlivre's *THE WONDER: A
WOMAN KEEPS A SECRET*.
Rowe's *JANE SHORE*.

1715
Jacobite Rebellion.
Death of Tate.
Rowe made Poet Laureate.

Married to a young woman though
in ill health.
Death on December 31.

1716
Addison's *THE DRUMMER*.

1717
David Garrick born.
Cibber's *THE NON-JUROR*.
Gay, Pope, and Arbuthnot's
*THREE HOURS AFTER MAR-
RIAGE*.

1718
Death of Rowe.
Centlivre's *A BOLD STROKE
FOR A WIFE*.

1719
Death of Addison.
Defoe's *Robinson Crusoe* published.
Young's *BUSIRIS, KING OF
EGYPT*.

1720
South Sea Bubble.
Samuel Foote born.
Steele suspended from the Gover-
norship of Drury Lane (restored
1721).
Little Theatre in the Haymarket
opened.
Steele's *The Theatre* (periodical)
published.
Hughes' *THE SIEGE OF DAMAS-
CUS*.

1721
Walpole became first Minister.

1722
Steele's *THE CONSCIOUS LOVERS.*

1723
Death of Susannah Centlivre.
Death of D'Urfey.

1725
Pope's edition of Shakespeare published.

1726
Death of Jeremy Collier.
Death of Vanbrugh.
Law's *Unlawfulness of Stage Entertainments* published.
Swift's *Gulliver's Travels* published.

1727
Death of George I; accession of George II.
Death of Sir Isaac Newton.
Arthur Murphy born.

1728
Pope's *The Dunciad* (first version) published.
Cibber's *THE PROVOKED HUSBAND* (expansion of Vanbrugh's fragment *A JOURNEY TO LONDON*).
Gay's *THE BEGGAR'S OPERA.*

1729
Goodman's Fields Theatre opened.
Death of Congreve.
Death of Steele.
Edmund Burke born.

1730
Cibber made Poet Laureate.
Oliver Goldsmith born.
Thomson's *The Seasons* published.
Fielding's *THE AUTHOR'S FARCE.*

Fielding's *TOM THUMB* (revised as *THE TRAGEDY OF TRAGEDIES*, 1731).

1731
Death of Defoe.
Fielding's *THE GRUB-STREET OPERA*.
Lillo's *THE LONDON MERCHANT*.

1732
Covent Garden Theatre opened.
Death of Gay.
George Colman the elder born.
Fielding's *THE COVENT GARDEN TRAGEDY*.
Fielding's *THE MODERN HUSBAND*.
Charles Johnson's *CAELIA*.

1733
Pope's *An Essay on Man* (Epistles I–III) published (Epistle IV, 1734).

1734
Death of Dennis.
The Prompter began publication (1734–1736).
Theobald's edition of Shakespeare published.
Fielding's *DON QUIXOTE IN ENGLAND*.

1736
Fielding led the "Great Mogul's Company of Comedians" at the Little Theatre in the Haymarket (1736–1737).
Fielding's *PASQUIN*.
Lillo's *FATAL CURIOSITY*.

1737
The Stage Licensing Act.
Dodsley's *THE KING AND THE MILLER OF MANSFIELD*.
Fielding's *THE HISTORICAL REGISTER FOR 1736*.